City Riffs

**Urbanism
Ecology
Place**

For my students.
— R.P.

Richard Plunz

City Riffs

Urbanism
Ecology
Place

Columbia University GSAPP

Lars Müller Publishers

ACKNOWLEDGMENTS

This collection has been culled from numerous texts involving a broad range of city involvements. It owes much to those cities and their constituent advocates who in effect are collaborators in this effort. I shall thank several. For Antwerp and Brussels, I am indebted to my colleagues at the Katholieke Universiteit Leuven, Bruno DeMeulder, Marcel Smets, Andre Loeckx, Hilde Heynen, and Lieven DeCauter. For Detroit I am indebted to Camilo Vergara and Stephen Vogel; for Manhattan to Geert Bekaert and Manuel de Solà Morales; for Caracas to Carlos Gomez de Llarena and Allan Brewer-Carias; for Mostar to Amir Pašić; for Prague to Alexandra Bravcová and Radomír Šofr; for Troy to Robert Winne; for Salzburg to Hubert Klumpner and Barbara Wally; for Seoul to Seoyong Kim; for Brooklyn to Linda LaViolette and the late Betty Stoltz; for Larderello to Paolo Pietrogrande; for Rome to Cinzia Abbate and Maria Paola Sutto; for Kumasi to Susan Blaustein and Beldina Opiyo-Omolo; for New Delhi to Viren Brahmbhatt and Geeta Mehta; for Turgutreis to Suha Özkan and Doruk Pamir.

At Columbia University, where much of this work originated, I have exchanged ideas with faculty and students during my years as Director of the Urban Design Program; I am grateful for many other involvements with the Architecture, Urban Planning, and Historic Preservation programs, as well as with the Urban Design Lab at the Earth Institute. Of particular importance has been my long collaboration with Patricia Culligan from Engineering, in both the Urban Ecology Studio and in the Urban Design Lab, with many colleagues and students in engineering. To Dean Bernard Tschumi I am indebted for his encouragement in 1992 to reinvent the Urban Design Program; and to Mojdeh Baratloo for her support and energy early on. I also acknowledge the encouragement of Dean Amale Andraos and Kenneth Frampton in completing this project.

Numerous architecture and urban design students have assisted in preparing this volume, including Amy Shell, A.L. Hu, and Steven Kyle-Cook. Above all I am indebted to Eleni Gklinou for her participation in all aspects of the final preparation, including the illustrations. The contributions of Lars Müller and his publication team, including Esther Butterworth, have been greatly appreciated. Finally, James Graham, Director of Publications, together with Isabelle Kirkham-Lewitt and Jesse Connuck, have made completion of this initiative a pleasure.

— R.P.

The Cause of the City

By Kenneth Frampton

There are no more cities, in fact, anymore. It goes on like a forest.
That is the reason why we cannot have the old cities anymore;
that is gone forever, planned city and so on. We should think about
the means that we have to live in a jungle, and maybe we will
do well by that.

— Mies van der Rohe, 1955[1]

Throughout his tenure as the director of the Urban Design program at the Graduate School of Architecture, Planning, and Preservation, Columbia University, Richard Plunz's position toward the predicament of the late modern city has been self-consciously cosmopolitan, as is borne out by this anthology of case studies testifying to the difficulty of projecting and realizing significant urban form in the twenty-first century, at a moment when wholesale urbanization continues worldwide with ever increasing intensity. Each of these short texts, written between 1993 and 2014, is a disquisition on the demise of the bourgeois city, that legacy of the medieval burgher class that first gave the city its name. It is significant in this regard that Plunz begins with the city of Antwerp and, moreover, with its cathedral, prefaced, as is the case with each of these essays, by a black-and-white figure-ground plan of the civic fragment under consideration, which in this instance is an aerial plan of Antwerp cathedral, an instance of Bruno Taut's concept of *Die Städtkrone* (City Crown) of 1919, without which a city, in the strictest sense, could not be deemed to exist. Such a *parti pris* could hardly be further removed from the highly toxic instrumental relic of the Gowanus Canal in Brooklyn, which is the focus of one of the case studies, exemplifying a quintessential brownfield site subject to endless remediation.

9

Part memoir, part reportage, with the genre alternating as one passes from one entry to the next, these essays and interviews tend to oscillate between being a specific critique of a particular situation and an overarching requiem for the lost cause of the city as the ultimate cradle of civilization. Sooner or later, in every instance, Plunz's analysis comes to the same conclusion, namely, that the city and the consumer society are mutually incompatible, just as maximizing the consumption of nonrenewable resources and the attendant phenomena of global warming, rising sea levels, flash floods, drought, and out-of-control wildfires are all inextricably connected.

Participating as a student and as an architect in the post-Second World War social-democratic promise of the 1960s, a moment in which the world and the potential of a reconstructive urbanism could have taken a different turn, Plunz was profoundly influenced by the seemingly liberative discourse of Team 10, and it is to this that he still turns, even now, as the Archimedean point from which to confront the political paralysis of both the United States and the world in general, as they both enter further into the unsustainable, vicious circle of optimized consumption; witness the recent project of the Chinese Communist Party to urbanize three hundred fifty million peasants over the next decade in order to create a consumer society.

These are the writings of a critical intellectual, and in this regard we should acknowledge the strategic models and the modes of beholding that have influenced his thought: above all, Serge Chermayeff and Christopher Alexander's model of low-rise, high-density housing as this was expressly envisaged for the Eastern Seaboard of the United States, as we find this in their book *Community and Privacy* of 1964. A second decisive influence was E. J. Mishan's seminal book *The Costs to Economic Growth* of 1967, wherein a radical economist first advances the case that the very concept of continual growth as the fundamental mechanism of capitalist accumulation is in and of itself unsustainable. As Plunz notes, Mishan's book would anticipate much of the material explored in the 1972 publication *The Limits to Growth: A Report to the Club of Rome on the Predicament of Man,* the two works together amounting to an indictment of globalization *avant la lettre.* This condition is increasingly confirmed today by the growing maldistribution of wealth and by the seemingly irreversible decay of our grossly overextended automotive infrastructure. Given the Disneyfication of the historic city in the service of tourism and the undermining of main street in the provincial city through the proliferation of the suburban shopping center, one of the only remedial options still available today would seem to be the densification of our present patterns of land settlement in order to arrive at a catchment of density sufficient to support some form of public transport and, at the same time, to reduce the wanton consumption of agricultural land, which, as of now, amounts to three million acres a year lost to suburbanization in the United States alone.

As Plunz makes clear in his preface and footnotes, there are many other authors who have influenced his work over the years, including figures as familiar in the world of environmental culture as Lewis Mumford, Fernand Braudel, Marshall McLuhan, Michel Foucault, Fredric Jameson, Ian McHarg, Bernard Rudofsky, Naomi Klein, Bill McKibben, and above all, of course, Henri Lefebvre, whose seminal book *The Production of Space* of 1974 remains a classic in the field.

Plunz's anthology ends at another pole entirely from the cathedral with which it opens. The final essay addresses the place of Turgutreis on the Turkish Aegean coast, which, when Plunz first visited the site in 1974, consisted of nothing more than three small villages. One of these, the village of Karabağ, is rendered here as a sparsely occupied figure-ground frontispiece, standing in for the seemingly unrepresentable conglomeration of present-day Turgutreis, comprising, as it does, a dense complex of luxurious vacation homes, condominiums, and hotels, housing a year-round population of twenty-three thousand and a summer population of two hundred fifty thousand, as opposed to the former village population of less than twenty-five hundred. Over the years Plunz led a number of different study teams, which passed from making a record of that which was still, forty years ago, a time-honored rural way of life, to a consideration of the kind of hybrid development that might have been enabled by something of its rooted, rural civilization, to coexist with the transformation of the coast into a vacation destination. In retrospect, as Plunz concedes, such a balanced compromise at the level of policy proved to be unattainable.

It is significant that the last of the new towns in both the United States and the United Kingdom, namely Milton Keynes and Reston, should coincide with the rise of neoliberalism in both countries, with the result that today we are left, as this anthology implies, with the aporetic question as to what possible limit or scope may be meaningfully ascribed to the task of urban design.

---

1 Ludwig Mies van der Rohe, transcript of interview with John Peter, 1955, Library of Congress, 14–15.

Field Urbanism

If this volume represents a psychogeography of cities and situations, so, too, does it represent a web of movements, ideas, and texts. Involved is an eclectic legacy, determined by moment, chance, and design. It wanders like the *flâneur* of Baudelaire and Benjamin, but through concepts and words as much as through streets. My web is diverse—a kind of *dramatis personae* embedded as an eclectic canon meandering among the many thinkers who have rested on my shelves over the years. They are a Moloch-like presence that weaves in and out of consciousness through these fragments or "riffs," the detritus from many years of researching "urbanism."[1] Above all else their contribution reflects on the importance of place.

As an exercise in urban forensics, these fragments also weave a *dramatis civitas*, a "moveable feast" through an array of citizens and situations. They describe liminal city moments as critical thresholds between urban phenomena, and they address global urban constituents with shared urban ideals. They demonstrate that cities share more than nations.

What is implied in these texts is affirmation of the importance of empirical evidence in defining the *urban* in its multitude of facets. In grappling with this question, Henri Lefebvre has been a prominent figure in my *dramatis personae*. Lefebvre portrays empirical evidence as both "*of* the urban (inside an emergent urban universe) and *about* the urban (describing it, outlining its contours)." This distinction between *of* and *about* lies at the heart of my understanding of the limitations in recording urban field phenomena. He acknowledges "this kind of discourse can never be completed. Its incompletion is an essential part of its existence." And he points to another limitation: that discourse is necessarily selective, such that "...ideology has played a large part in the development of a body of doctrine known as urbanism. To continue our exploration of the blind field, we had to jettison that opaque, heavy body; the urban phenomenon in its totality."[2] Although I have learned much from the natural sciences, urbanism engages social science factors beyond the boundaries of the normative "natural." This spatial and social nexus is messy, in effect Lefebvre's "ideology."

The protocols of field urbanism do not appear to have evolved to the same degree as field ecology, such that field ecology can anticipate a certain convergence.[3] The "urban" and the "ecological" share concepts of place. While place-based pedagogy has long been central to professional training in urbanism, the notion of place has nonetheless escaped the same theoretical scrutiny as in the environmental sciences.[4] Place-based pedagogy has engaged a long evolution in the natural sciences, and in many respects can serve as a model for advancing a field-based urbanism.[5] In some sense what is shared between the two realms may be diversity; biological diversity merges with urban diversity, following the logic that place always remains a philosophical centering. Field urbanism cannot simply "observe." There can be no pretense of "neutrality." Field urbanism requires context forensics that accept this condition—layers of subtlety and ambivalence that are essential to understanding. In my journey through this array of city moments, confronting the constraints of empiricism and a certain disciplinary ambivalence surrounding the question of spatial design have proven to be essential. This inevitability makes for improvisation or "riffs," albeit with a hint of Piranesi's Campo Marzio.

The biologist Edward O. Wilson refers to cities as the "greatest of machines," and if the common aphorism holds that indeed cities are the "natural" habitat of humankind, then by implication the "urban," the "natural," and the "machine" are not dialectically opposed.[6] Urban ecologies, however, are not totally analogous to natural ecologies. Cities are ecosystems that require intense biophilic relationships with their citizens, relationships that are difficult to disengage. In this regard, the city is no longer the historical entity that we have been acculturated to envision, no longer a kind of protective medieval citadel.[7] The city is not a redoubt against nature but quite the opposite. And if, in the words of Ulrich Beck, "nature is not nature, but rather a concept, norm, memory, utopia, counter-image...," cities are an essential component of our global ecosystem.[8] Urban infrastructure and politics must incubate this new worldview, especially as the Anthropocene unfolds.

For urbanism, the Epicurean continuum from "void to place to room" seems as useful today as it was two millennia ago.[9] It directly implicates spatial design, raising the question "Who is the designer?" Place and room are intrinsic to architecture and urban design practice, although these diverse disciplinary boundaries may be blurry relative to each other and to other fields, including engineering. Turfs can be in contention, within and without the design disciplines. The design disciplines, like other disciplines, have passed through post-structuralist phenomenological transitions.[10] For urbanism, the transition from structuralism to phenomenology was already noted by Lefebvre in 1970:

> There is no model for determining the urban through its elements or conditions (what it brings together—contents and activities). Models borrowed from the fields of energy (devices that capture finite, but considerable quantities of energy) and information (which uses minute amounts of energy) are also inappropriate here. In other words, if we want to find a model, an analytic study of the urban can supply them. But in practice, this has more to do with a path (sense and direction, orientation and horizon) than a model.[11]

For urbanism, however, things have not evolved to the same degree as in the natural sciences. And for urbanism, the social sciences are engaged beyond the normative "natural"—Lefebvre's "sense and direction" may be as close as we can come to a model or theory. Given evolving behavioral dimensions in field urbanism research, both "hard" and "soft" sciences are in play. Engineers, architects, and technicians must incubate new strategic relationships with ecological science within the broad perspective of eco-criticism.[12] All ecological disciplines have experienced similar transitions, for example, the emergence of "eco-criticism," which relates the sensibilities of literary criticism to ecology. This "literary city" provides vital cognitive evidence throughout the history of what has been, what is, and what can be.[13]

With the post-structuralist transition, cognate processing gained prominence in field urbanism. Kevin Lynch's contributions in the 1960s were seen as significantly expanding the processes of mapping, explored however tenuously in various other ways including the Situationist *dérive* and its adherents. Some did not find this approach robust enough. Fredric Jameson, for example, characterized *The Image of the City* as having "spawned the whole lowlevel [sic] subdivision that today takes the phrase 'cognitive mapping' as its own destination"—devoid of "any conception of political agency or historical process... locked within the limits of phenomenology."[14] Jameson points to unraveling the syntax of urban language as a challenge and to cognition as a crucial tool in this endeavor. And our advances in social media make new cognitive tools the next frontier.

Field urbanism is cognition and it is mapping, and it suffers similar limitations as field ecology. In this regard, the pragmatics of the evolution of modern ecological science can shed light on our language and syntax dilemmas, beginning with Darwin and his famous metaphor of the "entangled bank," which engages the challenge of seeing:

> It is interesting to contemplate an entangled bank, clothed with many plants of many kinds, with birds singing on the bushes, with various insects flitting about, and with worms crawling through the damp earth, and to reflect that these elaborately constructed forms, so different from each other, and dependent on each other in so complex a manner, have all been produced by laws acting around us.[15]

Darwin's metaphor raises forensic questions parallel to those in urbanism—the "entangled bank" is also the "entangled city." And here, too, we have urban place as an "entangled bank." Just as field ecology entails the search for place-based models, so does field urbanism.

It is useful to link our understanding of field urbanism to the concepts of ecologist Aldo Leopold, whose admonition "think like a mountain" resonates for cities. In his essay of the same name, Leopold views the whole of an infinite ecosystem, in all its complexity, from a vantage point on a mountain. From this position, he considers not only the participation of the viewer but the process of ecological succession, from the constellations of the night sky to a dying wolf's eyes.[16] Leopold's thinking lies at the beginnings of the "deep ecology" movement, connecting nature with spirituality and arguing for deeper understandings of ecological systems beyond the limitations of hard science.[17] And from this sensibility springs Felix Guattari's explication of the "Third Ecology" of social intercourse.[18] "Evolution" in the Darwinian sense is vastly more complicated for an "ecosophy" that engages a society intimately interconnected with nature within the context of a global "reflexive modernization." Leopold's "mountain" now meets Ulrich Beck's "risk society" with its commodification of risk now vastly more globalized than at any period in our evolutionary past.[19] And now with a planet projected to be 64 percent urbanized by 2050.[20]

Which leads us back to our *dramatis civitas* of city, place, and circumstance and our understanding of just how much cities must share given the growing affinity of needs across cities from diverse geographic and economic contexts. The new and cutting-edge infrastructural tools, for example, that equally apply to Kumasi in Ghana and Brooklyn in New York have a similar genesis: the changing economic and ecological realities of each context. New York City cannot replicate the large-scale infrastructural moves that fostered its rapid growth in the nineteenth century—its single-pipe combination of both raw sewage and storm water is not an option for twenty-first-century norms, and a second pipe is prohibitively costly. Kumasi has no pipe at all. For both cities a third option without pipes is needed, and it will arrive in the form of fine-grain distributed systems for water management, as well as for Lefebvre's "energy" and "information" systems. These new systems will be networked by new social media as a "bottom-up" necessity. Essential to these considerations is the idea of repetitive operations—and the understanding that large scale is also incrementally small scale. Large-impact infrastructural moves can be accomplished by repetitive small units, augmenting old top-down development models partially or completely.

Within our "urban universes" the needs of two places as diverse as Kumasi and Brooklyn intersect. Cities have as much to say to each other as nations do. Urban dwellers are world citizens able to "think like mountains." World culture is urban culture. Urban ecologies are biophilic. No intellectual and operative enterprise is more complicated than engaging the city within our own cognitive development. These text fragments offer a glimpse of our "mountain." And if there is a "deep ecology," so surely it follows that there is a "deep urbanism."

1 The following are representative texts in reference to the *dramatis personae* to serve as a canonical sequence for definition of a place-based field urbanism: Susanne Langer, *Philosophy in a New Key; a Study in the Symbolism of Reason, Rite, and Art* (1961); Benjamin Lee Whorf, *Language, Thought, and Reality: Selected Writings* (1967); Marshall McLuhan, *Understanding Media: The Extensions of Man* (1964); Ross Ashby, *Design for a Brain: The Origin of Adaptive Behavior* (1960); Norbert Wiener, *Cybernetics or Control and Communication in the Animal and the Machine* (1961); Colin Cherry, *On Human Communication: A Review, a Survey, and a Criticism* (1961); Anatol Rapoport, *Operational Philosophy: Integrating Knowledge and Action* (1961); Melvin Webber, ed., *Explorations into Urban Structure* (1964); Richard L. Meier, *A Communications Theory of Urban Growth* (1962); Harold Proshansky et al., eds., *Environmental Psychology: Man and His Physical Setting*

(1970); Michel Foucault, *The Archaeology of Knowledge & The Discourse on Language* (1972); Fredric Jameson, *The Prison-House of Language: A Critical Account of Structuralism and Russian Formalism* (1972); Henri Lefebvre, *Everyday Life in the Modern World* (1971); David Harvey, *Explanation in Geography* (1969); Edward Soja, *Postmodern Geographies: The Reassertion of Space in Critical Social Theory* (1989); Neil Smith, *Uneven Development: Nature, Capital, and the Production of Space* (1984); Lieven De Cauter, *The Capsular Civilization: On the City in the Age of Fear* (2004); Oscar Lewis, *La Vida: A Puerto Rican Family in the Culture of Poverty—San Juan and New York* (1966); Aldo Van Eyck, *Aldo Van Eyck: The Shape of Relativity* (1998); Marcel Griaule, *Conversations with Ogotemmêli: An Introduction to Dogon Religious Ideas* (1965); Amos Rapoport, *House Form and Culture* (1969); Bernard Rudofsky, *Architecture without Architects* (1964); Lewis Mumford, *The City in History: Its Origins, Its Transformations, and Its Prospects* (1961); Jane Jacobs, *The Death and Life of Great American Cities* (1961); Serge Chermayeff and Christopher Alexander, *Community and Privacy: Toward a New Architecture of Humanism* (1963); Shadrach Woods, *The Man in the Street: A Polemic on Urbanism* (1975); Ian McHarg, *Design with Nature* (1969); Patrick Geddes, *Cities in Evolution* (1950); Benton MacKaye, *The New Exploration: A Philosophy of Regional Planning* (1962); Ezra J. Mishan, *The Costs of Economic Growth* (1967); Donella H. Meadows, et al., *The Limits to Growth: A Report for the Club of Rome's Project on the Predicament of Mankind* (1972); Christopher Alexander, *Notes on the Synthesis of Form* (1964); Christian Norberg-Schulz, *Existence, Space & Architecture* (1971); Kevin Lynch, *What Time Is This Place?* (1972); Gianfranco Caniggia and Gian Luigi Maffei, *Architectural Composition and Building Typology: Interpreting Basic Building* (2001); Aldo Rossi, *The Architecture of the City* (1982); Manfredo Tafuri, *Architecture and Utopia: Design and Capitalist Development* (1976); Giancarlo De Carlo, *Urbino: The History of a City and Plans for Its Development* (1970); Stephen Wolfram, *A New Kind of Science* (2002); P. D. Ouspensky, *A New Model of the Universe: Principles of the Psychological Method in Its Application to Problems of Science, Religion, and Art* (1967).

2 Henri Lefebvre, *The Urban Revolution* (Minneapolis, MN: University of Minnesota, 2003), 166.

3 There are many manuals on procedural practice in field ecology. For example, see C. Philip Wheater, James R. Bell, and Penny A. Cook, *Practical Field Ecology: A Project Guide* (Hoboken, NJ: Wiley, 2011).

4 The evolving sophistication of place-based pedagogy in ecological science is demonstrated in the essays found in Ian Billick and Mary V. Price, *The Ecology of Place: Contributions of Place-based Research to Ecological Understanding* (Chicago: University of Chicago, 2010). Also see William Edelglass, "Philosophy and Place-Based Pedagogies," in *Teaching Philosophy,* ed. Andrea Kenkmann (New York: Continuum, 2009). See especially Chapter 2, Sharon E. Kingsland, "The Role of Place in the History of Ecology."

5 For urbanism, see Edward S. Casey's studies on place-based concepts: Edward S. Casey, *The Fate of Place: A Philosophical History* (Berkeley: University of California, 1997); Edward S. Casey, *Getting Back into Place: Toward a Renewed Understanding of the Place-world* (Bloomington, IN: Indiana University Press, 1993). Also see Ian Billick and Mary V. Price, *The Ecology of Place: Contributions of Place-based Research to Ecological Understanding* (Chicago: University of Chicago, 2010).

6 Edward O. Wilson, *Biophilia* (Cambridge, MA: Harvard University Press, 1984), 12.

7 The historical relationships between cities and agriculture are a key ecological consideration in urbanism. For medieval nature, see chapter eight of Fernand Braudel, *The Structures of Everyday Life: The Limits of the Possible,* vol. 2 of *Civilization and Capitalism 15th–18th Century* (Berkeley: University of California Press, 1992); also see chapter seven of David J. Herlihy, "Attitudes toward the Environment in Medieval Society," in *Historical Ecology: Essays on Environment and Social Change,* ed. Lester J. Bilsky (Port Washington, NY: Kennikat, 1980).

8 Ulrich Beck, *Ecological Politics in an Age of Risk,* trans. Amos Weisz (Cambridge, UK: Polity, 1995), 38.

9 See chapter four of Casey, *The Fate of Place: A Philosophical History.*

10 Much has been written on phenomenology and architecture, including the useful account of my Columbia colleague Jorge Otero-Pailos, *Architecture's Historical Turn: Phenomenology and the Rise of the Postmodern* (Minneapolis, MN: University of Minnesota, 2010), especially the epilogue. See also Charles S. Brown and Ted Toadvine, eds., *Eco-phenomenology: Back to the Earth Itself* (Albany, NY: State University of New York, 2003).

11 Lefebvre, *The Urban Revolution,* 175.

12 Cheryll Glotfelty, ed., *The Ecocriticism Reader: Landmarks in Literary Ecology* (Athens, GA: University of Georgia, 1996).

13 For urban literary naturalism, see Christophe Den Tandt, *The Urban Sublime in American Literary Naturalism* (Urbana, IL: University of Illinois Press, 1998).

14 Fredric Jameson, "Cognitive Mapping," in Cary Nelson and Lawrence Grossberg, eds., *Marxism and the Interpretation of Culture* (Urbana, IL: University of Illinois, 1988), 347–60. The field entails

far more than Lynch's approach. For useful overviews, see Rob Kitchin and Scott Freundschuh, ed., *Cognitive Mapping: Past, Present, and Future* (London and New York: Routledge, 2000) and Tommy Garling, ed., *Urban Cognition* (London and San Diego: Academic, 1995).

15 Charles Darwin, *The Annotated Origin: A Facsimile of the First Edition of On the Origin of Species/Charles Darwin* (Cambridge, MA: Belknap Press, 2009), 489. For this aspect of Darwin's influence, see Joel B. Hagen, *The Entangled Bank: The Origins of Ecosystem Ecology* (New Brunswick, NJ: Rutgers University Press, 1992). Also see Stanley Edgar Hyman, *The Tangled Bank: Darwin, Marx, Frazer and Freud as Imaginative Writers* (NY: Atheneum, 1962), 26–43.

16 Aldo Leopold, *A Sand County Almanac & Other Writings on Ecology & Conservation*, ed. Kurt Meine (New York: Library of America, 2013), 114–17. The importance of Leopold within the environmental movement is well summarized in Rory Spowers, *Rising Tides: A History of the Environmental Revolution and Visions for an Ecological Age* (Edinburgh: Canongate, 2002), 56–60.

17 The "deep ecology" movement in literature is well represented in Alan Drengson and Yuichi Inoue, eds., *The Deep Ecology Movement: An Introductory Anthology* (Berkeley: North Atlantic, 1995); and in George Sessions, ed., *Deep Ecology for the Twenty-First Century* (Boston: Shambhala, 1995). Also see George Sessions and Bill Devall, *Deep Ecology* (Layton, UT: Gibbs M. Smith, 1985). Leopold's role in the movement is described in Frederic L. Bender, *The Culture of Extinction: Toward a Philosophy of Deep Ecology* (Amherst, NY: Humanity, 2003), 315–18.

18 Felix Guattari, *The Three Ecologies*, trans. Ian Pindar and Paul Sutton (London and New Brunswick, NJ: Athlone, 2000). The effect of Hurricane Katrina on New Orleans is perhaps the most extreme example of Guattari's hypothesis. See John Protevi, "Katrina," in *Deleuze/Guattari & Ecology*, ed. Bernd Herzogenrath (Basingstoke, UK and New York: Palgrave Macmillan, 2009).

19 On the global manufacture of "risk" and its lack of social accountability, see Ulrich Beck, *Risk Society: Towards a New Modernity*, trans. Mark Ritter (London and Newbury Park, CA: Sage Publications, 1992). Also see Scott Lasch, Bronislaw Szerszynski, and Brian Wynne, eds., *Risk, Environment & Modernity* (London and Thousand Oaks, CA: Sage Publications, 1996).

20 As of 2014, the United Nations projected an increase of urbanites from 3.9 billion to 6.4 billion in 2050, or 64 percent of the total. United Nations, Department of Economic and Social Affairs, Population Division (2014). *World Urbanization Prospects: The 2014 Revision* (ST/ESA/SER.A/366).

Thinking about Antwerp and the Ideal of *Metropole*

Excerpted from "Thinking about Antwerp and the Ideal of *Metropole*," and "Against the Fear of Form," in *Taking Sides. Antwerp's 19th-Century Belt: Elements for a Culture of the City,* ed. Pieter Uyttenhove (Antwerp: Open Stad, 1993), 324–340, 357–358.

Antwerp, Cathedral Square

Meanwhile, since my business required it, I went to Antwerp...
— Thomas More, *Utopia*, Book I, 1516

Antwerp has always held a certain mystique for me. I remember reading More's *Utopia* in school and how the author begins at the cathedral. If we can believe historian Fernand Braudel, the cathedral was, at that moment, at the center of the city, which was at "the center of the entire international economy."[1] I remember having the feeling that perhaps Antwerp was more interesting than More's antithesis in *Utopia*. Of course my knowledge of this place developed as a consequence of my own teaching in Leuven, and it strikes me as one of the most fascinating "living" historical centers in Europe. I must qualify this immediately. For me, much of the interest of Antwerp is in what is not happening there. In Antwerp there is resistance to the obvious and a certain contrariness that I do admire—a seeming resistance to the homogenization of culture in the defense of Flemish regionalism, and an affirmation of the value of urbanity. The city remains alive, a working place rather than a dead, or worse, reincarnated monument in the total grip of tourism and the like.

Intertwined somewhere within the self-image of the population of Antwerp is the ideal of the *Metropole*. It is a word that in the popular culture has been used interchangeably with the proper name Antwerp. To come from Antwerp or the *Metropole* was to be of the "mother city," mother to Flemish culture and mother to the very concept of the modern *urbs*, the cradle of capitalism and of the Western metropolis as it has been idealized since the Renaissance. Antwerp was present at the "beginning," a hegemony that it has never forgotten. According to Braudel, Antwerp was the "new world capital" in the mid-sixteenth century, such that it could be defined as the first modern hub of international capital. How significant it is that this self-image has remained throughout the centuries. Now the term *Metropole* is receding from popular usage, an atrophy that may be symptomatic of a deeper malaise. Self-image can be self-fulfilling. In this regard, the future of Antwerp's urbanism appears to be at a turning point. The redevelopment of large-scale sites seen as the detritus of the industrial era will seal the fate of the city's urbanism well into the millennium.

During various crucial moments in the history of Antwerp, vast physical projects were undertaken at a scale disproportionate to the size of the city. In the sixteenth century, when Antwerp became the first modern "world capital," the urbanistic response was profound: the construction of the fortifications alone led to the demolition of some 1,300 houses; at the same time this intervention stimulated reurbanization at an even greater scale.[2] In the nineteenth century, the vast commitment to the railroad totally transformed the sensibility of the city. In the twentieth century, the extension of the port was once again unprecedented in physical scale. Between 1910 and 1929, during this phenomenal expansion of the city, the port increased the surface area of its docks threefold.[3] The present-day port extensions, as well as the transformation to vehicular transport and the prevalence of the private automobile remain unfinished business for the city. These transformations go in tandem with the gradual abandonment of the older port and railyards.

An aspect of the myth of *Metropole* has been the civic will to accept the layering of history, and Antwerp is a city in which the layers as a whole are more interesting than the individual episodes. Each of the historical layers of Antwerp has been associated with a new scaling of space for which the morphology of the preceding practice could not be reassigned. Each time, questions of urbanism were raised, questions which continue to be asked today. In this regard, the future of the railyard between Stuivenberg and the Dam is of particular importance to future development. The site represents an urbanistic discontinuity that drastically affects Antwerp's identity and function. At one level, the railyards have always represented a breach in the city, one devoid of habitable building. But as livelihood, they proposed another way of engaging the fabric of the city. And they were also monumental in scale. Just as the cathedral is a monument to the fourteenth and fifteenth centuries, the basins and yards are monuments to the nineteenth and twentieth centuries. Their alteration is culture-rending. The yards should not be replaced by a discreet urbanism of gentrification.

Though the genesis and functioning of both the railroad and port were continual, the basins of the old port and the railyards of Stuivenberg have differing issues related to reuse. As an urban amenity the great artificial "pools" of the port are an irreplaceable resource that should be preserved. Over time the city will expand and accommodate itself to their continuing presence. If in the future they retain their function as a transport medium, so much the better. They can remain as "working monuments." On the other hand, the mandate for maintaining the functional presence of the railyards seems less compelling. They pose a fundamental question: can the monumental formal qualities of such an obsolete zone be remembered? And what form could the anonymity of an infill fabric take?

As important to the identity of any city, beyond the monument, is the anonymous fabric. In this regard, no two cities are ever exactly alike and, for example, it is ultimately the housing typologies, the character of the streets, and other physical expressions of daily life, that most profoundly inform the character of a particular urbanism. A sentimentalist reproduction of the "medieval" or even of the nineteenth-century anonymous fabric is out of the question.

We initially considered the strategy that perhaps the scale and dynamism of the rail tracks could somehow inform the fabric that would come to replace them. And to some extent that could be mandated by the linear nature of the Stuivenberg site itself, but this, too, as a prominent basis for a *parti* was soon relegated to the category of the banal. Indeed, as has always been the case in the evolution of any urbanism, the nature of the fabric turned more and more to program, and not so much to functional program, which, anyway, cannot be precisely known for such a large proposal. Rather, it turned to questions of a spatial program related to what Geert Bekaert has called "the promised land of the spirit that extends into both past and future." The question became what can be the spatial paradigm for this "settling of accounts with history"?[4] Then out of necessity a second question emerged, which was: "How can this history itself be defined and delimited?"

In regards to Antwerp's urbanism, perhaps the most basic question is "which history?" Popular historymaking has long propelled the legend of the "golden age" of Antwerp during its sixteenth-century role as the "world capital." In that epoch lies Antwerp's pivotal role at the inception of modern capitalism and by consequence, modern urbanism. For that moment, all roads led to Antwerp. But the formation of the modern city did not begin or end then. For example, in the nineteenth century, the importance of geography would again claim the foreground. The sea link with North America was augmented by the rail link with Eastern Europe. In recent decades this infrastructure has been reinforced by auto routes. Although the interest of the Antwerp ring road is considerable, little critical notice has been made to date.[5]

Critical to understanding Antwerp's urbanism today, is not the historic center in spite of its emblematic history, but rather the periphery and the question of recent history. Like most cities in the late twentieth century, the center and periphery represent an extreme divide. In Antwerp the center represents the mythical view: the city within walls, or in this case, within the ring auto route, which has replaced the walls. But it is the outer periphery that dominates, such that it cannot be engaged by accommodation. The importance of the battle between the two geographies cannot be overstated. There are countless symptoms of the waning of the inner city as life force, both in myth and in socioeconomic reality. In Antwerp, *urbs* must take an aggressive position versus suburban dispersal. And any talk of large projects would have to nurture this strategy if the ideal of *Metropole* is to survive.

The most recent symptom of anti-*Metropole* has been the completion of the new shopping mall at Wijnegem at the Antwerp periphery. It is Belgium's largest mall, with 170 shops spread over 37,000 square meters. The *Financial Times* sees a positive, the Wijnegem project as a "miracle" that represents a final break in the line of defense of Belgian city centers, which until now were able to veto such schemes. The *Times* hints at the consequences: "... property professionals believe there is a chance that other Belgian towns will be tempted to approve such developments, fueling what is already a healthy growth in the retail sector."[6] But ignored is the question of why not build such developments within the inner cities: within the ring, for example, with the scores of thousands of square meters available in the cast-off industrial-era sites.

The *Financial Times* also speculated that "if mainstream Flemish politicians and business people are to be believed, Flanders is on the brink of a new era of prosperity built on the same basis as the Flemish booms of the middle ages and of the sixteenth and seventeenth centuries: location and trade." With this the myth of the "golden age" becomes dangerous. These same politicians and businessmen might be well advised to look again at the history that they emulate. Braudel writes about Antwerp's earlier apex in the sixteenth century:

> All the same the city was an economic innocent: other people came knocking at the door, moved in and made her fortune for her. Antwerp did not set out to capture the world—on the contrary, a world thrown off balance by the great discoveries, and tilting towards the Atlantic, clung to Antwerp, *faute de mieux*. The city did not struggle to reach the visible pinnacle of the world, but woke up one morning to find itself there.[7]

Will the same somewhat less than enviable state of affairs come to pass again, without an aggressive counterstrategy, this time with far more at stake in terms of the integrity of the city's urbanism? The central dilemma is how to maintain city control of large-scale development opportunities within a culture that essentially upholds an ideal of "city-state" medievalism within the context of very powerful multinational capital.

What is the meaning of the new infusion of multinational capital for the concept of the *Metropole*, if one accepts the trend of peripheral dispersal, which seems to go hand in hand with this infusion? Manifest destiny may be manifest, but it can be directed. The forces at work at the periphery can be redirected toward the nineteenth century belt. This has proved to be precisely the kind of issue that design study should illuminate, in that no such strategy can avoid the question of formal invention. The very notion of transliterating a suburban building language to an urban context requires spatial typologies not yet extant. That need is obvious in a city that is contradicted by its periphery in every way. For example, there is the dominance of the bourgeois ideal of the automobile and the detached cottage, which seems to keep so much of the housing stock of the inner city in marginal use, or the physical obsolescence of the old center for commercial or even for residential initiative, except for the Fifth Column of tourism, which can ultimately damage more of the life of the city than it can preserve. This threat exists in the ample evidence in the empty houses and dearth of real habitation in the historic center. And it exists in equal evidence in the lines of automobiles that enter the city in the morning and leave the city at night, or even more so in those that never have to enter at all, made all the more incredulous by the rail net of Belgium, which is the densest in the world.

Moving to the question of the utility of our outsider presence in Antwerp's internal debates, clearly important material has been engaged. But there has been enormous reluctance to discuss urbanism as "form," which has been a curious prognosis considering how many architects have participated. More precisely, one could identify a "fear of form," which has tended to pervade much of our exchange, as if it is not equally valid to explore questions of the formal evolution of the city as it is to explore questions of economic development. It seems obvious that both kinds of discourse must be simultaneous and interactive. What is so threatening about beginning with design, about making propositions we all know can have a limited half-life and can even be thrown away at any time? It is the physical proposal that is key to the process of renewal, and one cannot have too many of these proposals. It is the physical image that provokes political consensus or the lack of consensus. This is tricky business in relation to the body politic, or even to so sophisticated a group as architects, for that matter. Scores of proposals are needed, and why not? Perhaps then the facile answers of the bankers and politicians would not seem so conclusive.

These considerations bring me to the cynical journalist from the *Gazet van Antwerpen*, who maintains that we have no interest in the social problems of Antwerp and that we apparently do not understand anything at all about Antwerp.[8] Among other things, the observer maintained that the project discussion neglected issues of context, and in Stuivenberg in particular, "The social problematic of the neighborhood left the ladies and gentlemen cold. The word did not even cross their lips." It is even true that perhaps the "social problems" of Stuivenberg seem minuscule in comparison with certain areas of New York. The implications of this perception were discussed at some length within our sessions, including the possibility that the term "social problem" could itself be close to a euphemism for social prejudice in this circumstance. In any event, it is quite possible that this journalist, like us, failed to understand anything about Antwerp, just as it is possible that we do not understand anything about New York. What is the point? Cynicism is a danger. Even more dangerous is a fear of the new, a fear of the foreign. Xenophobia leads nowhere. If our role has been none other, perhaps our deliberations have revealed how Antwerp sees itself, and to us has fallen the task of exposure.

1 Fernand Braudel, *The Perspective of the World*, vol. 3 of *Civilization and Capitalism 15th–18th Century* (New York: Harper, 1984), 143. Columbia's urban design studios were invited to work in Antwerp in Spring 1993 on abandoned rail and port infrastructure, and in 1994 on the redevelopment of the Petroleum Zuid brownfield.

2 Herman van der Wee, *The Growth of the Antwerp Market and the European Economy* (Den Haag: Springer Netherlands, 1963), 192–93.

3 F. Suykens, et al., *Antwerp, The New Spring* (Antwerp: MIM Publishing Co, 1991), 169.

4 Geert Bekaert, "Terra Incognita," *Archis* #1 (1993): 5.

5 Willem Jan Neutelings, "La Ringzone di Anversa," *Casabella* 53 (January 1989): 42–45.

6 Andrew Hill, "Bust will not follow Building Boom," *Financial Times*, March 1993, 10.

7 Braudel, *The Perspective of the World*, 145.

8 H. Verleyen, "Een alarmkreet en een luchtkasteel," *Gazet van Antwerpen*, May 1993, 33.

Detroit
Is Everywhere

"Detroit Is Everywhere," *Stadt Bauwelt* 127 (September 1995): 2,012–13; revised and republished as "Detroit Is Everywhere," *Architecture* 85 (April 1996): 55–61.

Detroit, Grand Circus

Detroit offers valuable lessons in urbanism at the end of the twentieth century. During the Cold War, the city achieved almost mythic status as the source of our cultural icons related to automobiles and music, and was at the center of the "American way of life." Then Detroit fell, its demise symbolized by the race riots of 1967. And though some might regard its situation as an extreme aberration of our urbanity, I maintain that Detroit is a reflection of our culture at large. Detroit is everywhere.

To look at Detroit is to look at all of our cities with the symptoms of our urban decline enhanced. And at the very least, the city is important as a very visible product of the economic and cultural transformations that began with the Great Depression over six decades ago.

The Depression signaled that the United States was no longer a "developing" country. The challenge was to maintain an expansionist economy in the face of matured industrial development. The success of this strategy depended on inventing a culture of consumption that could provide a marketplace for consumer products. As far as our existing cities were concerned, however, this new consumer culture could not flourish. "Urbanism as a way of life," to use American sociologist Louis Wirth's famous aphorism, had to be replaced by "suburbanism as a way of life." The new society, by definition, had to be a waste society. Urban proximity was the antithesis of waste. The nation had to be de-urbanized, and the key to this dispersal was the automobile.

The resulting physical and cultural de-urbanization of the United States has been a highly directed and intensive long-term process, which began in the 1930s with highways created by the Works Progress Administration and single-family cottage subsidies funded by the Federal Housing Administration. Flailing industrial giants experimented with their consumer products, readying themselves for the eventual recompense that would follow the interregnum of World War II. And the war itself created the requisite empire that could mortgage the future for the immediate gratification of American consumption. The essential catalyst was cheap gasoline, which today remains the lifeblood of the strategy.

Detroit's growth mirrored the success of new America. But even as it reached its pinnacle, Detroit was undermined by its machines. While the city was still needed to produce the automobile, the automobile's effect on the Motor City was destructive. The process was abetted by General Motors' removal of Detroit's trolleys in 1955, as workers could afford cars. The city became the archetype of consumerist urbanism. As such, Detroit fulfills the hypothesis of the French cultural theorist Guy Debord in *Society of the Spectacle* (1967): the city of consumption ultimately consumes itself.

While today, trolleys manufactured in Detroit run in Mexico City, Detroit itself offers virtually no public transportation. General Motors followed the same strategy in scores of U.S. cities. The force of this corporate power and self-assumed omnipotence was harshly revealed in 1952 with General Motors president Charles Wilson's famous reflection that "what was good for our country was good for General Motors, and vice versa." Now, in its own backyard, General Motors might be expected to face the urban consequences of its long consumerist odyssey—but when Detroit became useless to its makers, the companies that created it abandoned it. The capital became globalized beyond the spatial city.

The Detroit scenario has been played out in scores of other cities large and small, albeit in less cataclysmic terms. With the new global configuration of capital, the days of local urban patronage are gone. Gone is the era of reinvesting in cities the wealth that they have created: capital no longer has such localized obligations.

The national project for de-urbanization culminated in the 1990 census, which recorded a suburban majority for the first time in this nation's history. This new condition is a far cry from 1930, when the majority of the population was urban. American cities have been under siege ever since, the final *coup de grâce* coming with the intolerant Reagan revolution of the 1980s. Political power has shifted to the post-urbanites, and they are using it. Detroit's visibility is especially important now because it so completely epitomizes the consequences of the suburban condition.

For suburbanites, Detroit might as well stay exactly as it is. This sensibility is underlined by the racial dimension of the question. The city has the largest proportion of African Americans of any in the United States. Detroit openly exposes the American apartheid: white people reside safely in the suburbs while poor minorities live in the city—economic captives and inhabitants of a legacy that they cannot maintain or defend. We find this configuration in every other large city, but nowhere is it so brutal as in Detroit. The post-urbanites have colonized the city: Detroit has become a suburb of its suburbs.

By 1990, Detroit housed only half of its 1950 population of 1.8 million.[1] And within its tri-county region, its share of the population declined from more than 60 percent in 1950 to about 25 percent. Its urban automobile factories have been replaced by suburban distribution factories for the service industry, the purveyors of consumer culture. Detroit's residents must flow out of the city in search of work and goods, only to return to their own

Soweto—a situation aligning Detroit more and more with post-colonial attributes of the developing world.

Detroit is more Los Angeles than Los Angeles: no Metro, expressways with no exits, suburbs with no city, streets with no houses. There are crossroad "towns" at the center and "border crossings" at the periphery. Still, Detroit's urbanism somehow survives. It is a new urbanity. There are new infrastructures of itinerant paths; obsolete infrastructures of expressways with new meanings; new topographies of old houses. Already the new Detroit urbanism is evolving to a higher level of organism, transcending simple erasure.

A new scale and meaning of "monumentality" is embodied in the large collection of abandoned skyscrapers in downtown Detroit, the world's first such phenomenon. And there are the accretive transformations: for example, a parking garage housed in the lush, rococo auditorium of the Michigan Theater achieves a *poesis* beyond the banality of its expedience. In this, the post-structuralist theory of the past decade might do well to look at Detroit for its validation.

To understand Detroit, we must finally shed our expansionist illusions. Urban entropy is more important to current architectural theory and practice than urban "growth." If history itself is an urban construct, what survives in Detroit must challenge our idea of the city in history. Detroit offers a strange amalgam of proximity and emptiness—isolated pieces in proximity, but without propinquity.

Although one is reminded of the ebb and flow of medieval contractions, here the medieval has been sped up to an instant in history. Perhaps it is true that we are at the end of history. In this regard, we do not yet understand whether or not the *city*, as we have come to know it since the Renaissance, is still operative.

One suspects, however, that in spite of suburban majorities, the city is still the incubator of our economy and culture, and we cannot afford to discard it just yet. Just as we arrived at a "consumer" society, we will also arrive at a "post-consumer" society. In this regard, we can be certain of one thing: as goes the price of gasoline, so goes our cities. Mobil Oil recently advertised that gasoline is "America's best bargain." If so, it is a bargain that comes with an enormous real price in urbanistic terms.

---

1 The Detroit population has since dropped to almost one-third of this number. See Christine Mac-Donald, "Detroit Population Rank is Lowest Since 1850," *The Detroit News*, May 20, 2016. The Spring 1995 urban design studio was invited to work in Detroit, and a subsequent urban ecology studio in Fall 2015.

The Scale Canard?

Excerpted from "The Scale Canard?" *Daidalos* 61 (1996): 128–131.

Manhattan, Twin Towers

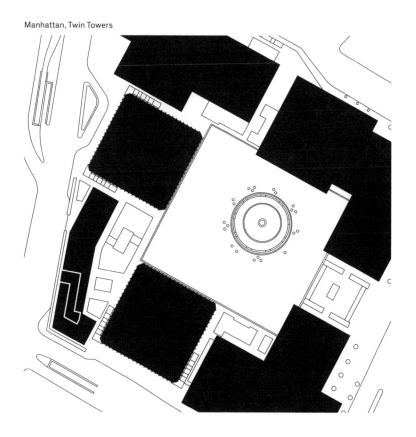

From my rooftop in Lower Manhattan, my eye wanders among the towers representing an interesting chronology of the type. The earliest and smallest are the most fantastic: the 1901 Broadway Chambers building (Cass Gilbert); the 1914 neoclassical Municipal Building (McKim, Mead and White) stands beyond it; and nearby, the 1913 Woolworth Building (Gilbert Cass), the "cathedral of commerce" and the tallest building in the world until the completion of the Empire State Building in 1932. The definitive scale is achieved by the twin towers of the 1972–73 World Trade Center (Minoru Yamasaki), which briefly displaced the Empire State Building as the tallest until the opening of the 1974 Sears Tower in Chicago. Behind the World Trade Center is the 1985 American Express headquarters (Cesar Pelli) symbolizing the era of cheap money, which is reflected on its transverse axis by the 1991 brick and glass spire of TriBeCa Tower (Schuman Lichtenstein Claman & Efron), the belated 1980s yuppie housing that bankrupted on the heels of the October 1987 market crash. This reliquary is rounded out by the classicist 1994 Federal Office Building (Hellmuth, Obata & Kassabaum), the most expensive and the most *retardataire* of the group. It is probably a banality to point out the possible readings of these buildings relative to economic and political power, yet there has been a recent outbreak of exactly such incitement from the media. The *New York Times* reasoned that never again will the "world's tallest" be built in the USA, while trying to put an upbeat spin on that depressing bit of news for the country.[1] But it is even true that American architects have not seemed to experience much difficulty exporting their high-rise wares: more success abroad than at home of late.

At the time of its completion, the World Trade Center seemed remarkable for its extraordinary architectural mediocrity contraposed with the fact that it could be built twice. On the one hand, it was an important expression of the economic power that New York City could still muster; on the other, an indication of the growing meaningless of the entire exercise. If it is possible to build two, why not build three or even a dozen? Much was made of the entry of building design itself into the "age of mechanical reproduction." This discussion now seems irrelevant, especially at night: one tower with its mast, the other with its observation deck and camera flashes every few seconds, often in clusters as tour groups move about the perimeter.

No one fails to read the towers as paeans to power. But fewer may remember them as the Rockefeller family's attempt to use government money to save their Lower Manhattan real estate from final oblivion, locally or globally. Their strategy was a dismal failure, instead delivering the final *coup de grâce* by helping drain the surrounding area. Lower Manhattan, once considered the bed-rock of world capitalism, has recently suffered an office vacancy rate of more than 25 percent, ranking among the highest in the country—a new scale record of sorts. The latest indignity is the luxury condo phase of reoccupation. Within this context there is even a proposal for developing a "Museum of the Skyscraper" in Lower Manhattan. In Las Vegas "Lower Manhattan" is being recon-structed as "New York–New York," a hotel and gambling casino: "high" and "low" culture at the end of the skyscraper era.

The tide first turned against the skyscraper in San Francisco in the late 1960s—and it turned for very good reasons, including the obvious ecological equations. By now, the tower has lost its allure in most U.S. cities, along with many other cultural relics dating from the height of "empire." But the exportation of these relics continues unabated, with shameless indifference to the so-called developing world relative to the hazards of the "Ameri-can way of life." Out there, the postcolonial mind-set requires the pursuit of these trophies at any cost. And so it is that the mantle now passes from the Sears Tower in Chicago to the twin Petronas Towers in Kuala Lumpur (Cesar Pelli and Associates), and by the year 2001 to the Shanghai World Financial Center (Kohn Pederson Fox). The Japanese, not to be outdone in their own backyard, study the possibility of a 300-story tower in Tokyo.

The present global rush for the highest skyscraper boils down to fetishistic ideas about "bigness" that transcend all rationality. This canard belies an underlying longer-term panic as we arrive at the final moments of the industrial era. The architectural scene accurately reflects this state of affairs. There is no other way to explain the critical acceptance of Rem Koolhaas' book *S,M,L,XL*, which markets the scale strategy at several levels, including the salvation of architecture itself:

> Beyond a certain scale, architecture acquires the properties of Big-ness. The best reason to broach Bigness is the one given by the climbers of Mount Everest: 'because it is there.' Bigness is ultimate architecture. It seems incredible that the size of a building alone embodies an ideological program, independent of the will of its architects ... Only Bigness instigates the regime of complexity that mobilizes the full intelligence of architecture and its related fields.[2]

The book itself, at 1,344 pages, is an extension of his argument—facilitated by digital graphics but constrained by the limitations of older binding technology.

No wonder Koolhaas can be so enamored with the mediocri-ty and incredible power of Wallace K. Harrison, palace architect to the Rockefellers and fantastic purveyor of the future. Like Harrison's, Koolhaas' work is significant as a period-piece reflection of such power, now for a second generation of post-industrial strategizing. Koolhaas fails to perceive that fighting scale with scale is a dead end. The post-industrial city is not consumptive of physical space as such. It differs from the extensive growth patterns formerly established by the industrial city, with its vast integration of factories and related infrastructure—railyards and port facilities, for example. The current panic to reuse old infrastructure is understandable especially given the political liabilities of contraction and abandonment—hence the tendency to fight the scale of abandonment with even more larger-scale spatial development. Nothing can be consumptive enough, however, and the consumerist nature of these programs is marginal relative to the fundamental global economic transformations that are under way. These entirely mediated environments are products of an ersatz socialism of a slightly provincial and politically ephemeral nature: "crowd-pleasing" in a phrase, for regions of labor obsolescence. Obsolescence of the social program, like the workforce, is a hallmark of the latest manifestation of the "city of consumption." One can imagine that in fifteen years, politicians and bankers may ruminate on what to do with Euralille, just as they did on the same site fifteen years ago.

The Western culture of architecture, like the culture at large, has been nurtured on an expansionist notion of building, which implies ever-increasing scale. In fact, now the opposite process of atrophy—"unbuilding"—is more and more important. Today, the process of removal is as important as that of addition, yet architects and urbanists are totally ill-equipped to deal with it from any point of view. Scale, and "business is business," is all that is left to the market, thus the deliberate dumping of obsolete technology from so-called "developed" to "developing" nations.

Within the realm of the built environment, this does not just include the relatively simple technologies of the "world's tallest" building. Far more consequential is the question of basic infrastructure. The problems facing Western urbanism, particularly in the period of postwar de-urbanization in the United States, can ill afford to be repeated on even larger scales elsewhere. In Asia, for example, we begin to see cities replicating the sprawl of Los Angeles and Phoenix on a scale far vaster: de-urbanization without automobiles, enforced by the ersatz socialism of centralized power in a region of labor commodification. Of course this can be a difficult issue, especially given the ideal of the "American way of life" that the global power of the U.S. media continues to promulgate. The antithesis of infrastructural investment is short-term profit.

36

Within the Western culture of architecture, it is fashionable to dismiss the relevance of "urban design," urban boundaries or even urban physicality itself, given the globalism of our spatial information systems. But that technology is precisely what feeds the spatial implosion—it is the global economy that stimulates local urbanization. The long-term social costs of an automobile built in Detroit or in Jakarta will be the same. This can be self-evident in visiting either city; in Detroit the world's largest collection of 1920s skyscrapers stands abandoned in the detritus of the industry that built it. In Jakarta, the 1991 Bank Niaga Tower (Kohn Pederson Fox Associates) stands next to an open sewage channel with an old kampong stretching beyond it. In both contexts, the scale of the towers is negligible; they are little more than chips in a casino game.

1 Paul Goldberger, "Why Cities Set Their Sights So High," *New York Times*, August 4, 1996.
2 Rem Koolhaas and Bruce Mau, *S,M,L,XL* (New York: Monacelli Press, 1995), 495–97.

The Conspiracy Against the City

Excerpted from "The Conspiracy Against the City: Lieven de Cauter in conversation with Richard Plunz," in *A Moving City*, ed. Veronique Patteeuw (Brussels: Studio Open City, 1998), 229–239.

Brussels, Mont des Arts

39

Lieven de Cauter: At the last Open City conference you made the following remarkable statement: "It is the city which is the natural habitat of men—not nature."[1] I had the impression that it was meant as a polemical statement against the audience, against the Belgian attitude towards the city, against a sort of deep-rooted anti-urban attitude. This is, of course, crystallized in the scale of negative responses to Brussels. Although it is more or less the only metropolitan space in Belgium, it arouses a range of feelings, moving from ignorance to indifference and fear up to dislike and hatred—all combined with an equally deep-rooted tendency towards the countryside and an unconditional love for the isolated, individual house. I took your blunt axiom that "the natural habitat of man is the city and not nature" to be a direct attack on this attitude.

> **Richard Plunz:** Not really. In fact, I had no ulterior motive. Although the statement that you quote functions quite well as a critique of the Belgian situation, and especially applies to the position of the Catholic Church.

LDC: The anti-urban Catholic policy is well known, and at the same time not known at all. It is still a public secret that there was a set policy to keep people in the countryside and in the provincial towns. The densest railroad network of Europe was installed to serve this goal: it was not just an innocent development. An intense rail network made it possible for people to stay in Bruges and work in Brussels, or even to stay in Bommerskonte and work in Brussels. The policy motivation behind this dispersal was not post-industrial; it was adopted during the Industrial Age in full blaze. The commuting mess in Brussels today is the result of this policy.

> **RP:** The interesting thing about this movement away from the city and "the little house problem" is that early on in the States a similar policy was promoted by the industrialists, whereas in Belgium it was apparently promoted more by the Catholic parties. But either way, an aspect of the attempts to keep people away from the city involved a moral strategy.

LDC: To keep people away from the city meant keeping them away from socialism, atheism, class, and other promiscuities and immoralities.

RP: In the States, however, dispersal was realized on a large scale with the post-industrial strategies of the '30s, which really involved economic planning. The program for a post-industrial consumer society could not be fully realized without suburbanization and de-urbanization. I think in Belgium this economic imperative wasn't discovered until quite late.

LDC: How do you mean "consumer society presupposes suburbanization?" Do you mean that there was a sort of conscious policy? Ford's slogan "every one his own car" is pointless for city dwellers? Is that what you mean?

RP: Yes. And while this strategy may seem evident, many people don't always want to see it as such. Consumer society and suburbanization go hand in hand.

LDC: I'm amazed when you say that the Catholic strategy can be compared to a post-industrial America (which means to me the '60s and after). But maybe this comparison between an anti-urban Catholic policy here and the suburbanization of America to realize a City of Consumption is too complex for this conversation. I would rather concentrate on your insinuation that there was a sort of conscious conspiracy against the city. You seem to suggest that the consumer society is deeply anti-urban and that this diaspora of the American population into endless suburbanization was a conscious strategy. Conspiracy theories always have a funny smell. Don't you overestimate the capitalist logic?

RP: No. Capitalist logic was there and it is still there. Housing and capitalism are inextricably linked. Everyone should want a house and to make it all more lucrative; there are the government tax policies and many kinds of monetary incentives to reinforce this desire. In the end it is all about money. If you buy a house, you make money. If you don't have the money to buy a house, you don't make money. It is a form of banking. In Belgium, maybe it is not so extreme.

LDC: It certainly is. I would even say that it is a national obsession. Let's concentrate, however, on the relation between city and countryside (or what is left of it). In Belgium, living and buying in the countryside is a lot cheaper than living and buying in the city, and this is the result of a policy, an absurd policy. Is it the same in the States?

41

RP: Absolutely. It costs double or triple to live in the city if you factor everything in: the suburbs enjoy enormous subsidies, the mortgage advantages, the costs of the roads, the subsidizing of the whole infrastructure. The entire value-system is orientated towards non-urbanity.

LDC: So you discover a strategy in all this?

RP: Yes, I do. However, I can't speak for the Belgian situation because I'm not familiar enough with the details. If you have lots of cottages in Belgium and huge motorways and a middle class wanting to be out of the city; it is quite the same formula as in the States. However, in the States it was a formula to renew the economy. We were once an urban country. Nobody says this anymore. In 1930 we had a higher proportion of urban population than France did. Government radically changed this ratio in two decades—in the '30s and '50s. In the post-industrial era, U.S. history has been rewritten in a way that presents American culture as having been anti-urban and basically rural, which is completely false.

LDC: Was it a conscious policy to make money? A sort of safe area for the middle class, while the city was considered a kind of ghetto?

RP: No, not at first. That happened a little later. The first imperative was to create a new economy after the collapse of 1929. The only way to make a new economy was to move to a consumer-dominated economy. Until then we were a "developing" country. But we reached the end of that era. The heavy industrial production of a developing country was in big trouble. It had to be transformed to another mode, and that is exactly what was done, in fact very well. It was certainly not an accident. I find it absurd when people argue that de-urbanization would have happened anyway. It could never have happened without massive government intervention. Government policy changed all the banking institutions, all the financing. It destroyed the entire economic infrastructure, and built new infrastructure. While all this is known, it is not generally accepted in recent urban discourse.

LDC: In Belgium we have similar processes. We have very dense infrastructure. But the train network, for instance, is not supporting the city. Instead it is supporting a huge commuter system. Since the train, we had a second wave of incredibly high density of motorways. Now we are saturated, and the problem is generated by policy. Everybody has to have and use a car to cover the smallest distance because public transport is weak and has even diminished over the years. But I'm not completely convinced that the policy was deliberate. It came partly as a *laissez-faire* liberal idea of giving the people what they wanted, and I think that people wanted to live in this ideal of a house in the countryside (which by this very process was, of course, turned into one huge suburbia stretching from Oostend to Genk). Even our politicians are middle-class people who want to live in a nice "villa."

> **Veronique Patteeuw:** If you look at the present condition of the city, do you think it is in danger? And if so, do you think it needs to be saved because of its qualities?

RP: When you look at cities, what is there? In the States there are a lot of serious intellectuals who argue that the traditional city simply doesn't exist anymore. I think they are wrong. I believe, indeed, that the natural habitat of humans is urban. This popular idea that the city is finished is a convenient one. If you consider the scale of the basic anti-urban operations of the post-war years, which was a huge investment, those responsible have to defend themselves.

LDC: So, you still see a capitalist conspiracy behind it?

RP: Of course.

LDC: Who are the bad guys?

> RP: The oil companies, for instance! We are willing to spend billions of dollars to threaten war on a global scale in order to maintain control of oil, in order to maintain our consumerist illusion. To me the situation seems completely obvious. I think the petrochemical age is basically anti-urban. The word "urbicide" has credibility. You can read it in the willful destruction of cities in war and also in normalized government policies. You can see urbicide on television every day. We even have

43

urban sitcoms made to be viewed by sub-urbanites that have completely lost urban contact. The secret of Disney—whether the urban village at Euro-Disney outside of Paris, or the operation now in New York on forty-second street and Times Square—is about creating virtual urban environments as a form of amusement.

LDC: The Disneyfication of the city, which is largely metaphorical, is not at all metaphorical in Times Square, however. This huge process of universally re-staging the post-industrial city as a theme park, is, according to your conspiracy theory, an importuned part of "urbicide"? I think you have a point there.

RP: I think we are at the end of a process. Therefore, I'm optimistic in the long-term. I don't believe "the end of the city" story at all. This kind of polemic is coming to an end. It has to.

LDC: Is this wishful thinking on your behalf?

RP: Yes.

LDC: Maybe we have a good, although ambiguous, sign of optimism in Brussels: what I call the "new mass." On a nice spring day Brussels is crowded—not only with foreign tourists, but also with people from outside and inside the city itself, a sort of mixture. You have the same thing with the cinema. For Brussels and Belgium, the cinema-chain of Kinepolis symbolized the end of the urban condition, as it destroyed the cinema culture of the city. It was the triumph of what we call the "ring-cultuur," the culture of the periphery, such that all the urbanites and suburbanites can come and mingle. However, as a reaction—and this is maybe a very small but very concrete sign of optimism—both in Brussels and Antwerp, there is now a reinvestment in cinemas in the city center. First there was a phase of closure, and now there is a massive reopening and revitalization of old cinemas. Maybe this is a kind of "new urbanity" (and yet it might be the vanguard of complete Disneyfication).

VP: Are there similar signs in New York?

RP: There are different ones. New York is experiencing huge reinvestments that I am a bit skeptical of. But yes, let's be optimistic for a minute or two. There is an enormous pressure for upper-middle and middle-income reoccupation of the city.

VP: A "new urban age?"

RP: Cities require a very micro-scale economic infrastructure. You have to be able to have single shops (as opposed to a global chain), because the very basis of urban fabric is connected to this level of urban activity. Sustaining the micro-scale is very difficult given the way the global economy is changing. You can order your products from the Internet for much cheaper, without ever stepping out onto the street. The unanswered question is are people still willing to go into the street and are they willing to pay a premium to still have the social amenity of the street?

LDC: So you are one of the few defenders of the old street?

RP: Yes, and I deliberately pay extra money to go into a shop, especially into the ones that I think deserve to be there. I think that in New York many people feel this way.

LDC: You are one of the few foreign observers of Brussels on a regular basis. If you look at Brussels—as you do—from a geopolitical point of view, what is your analysis? Have you noticed any changes during the past three years?

RP: To tell you the truth, I am not that optimistic for the moment. I don't see any real change in policies, for example. On the positive side, however, life is going on. I just don't see what you call a turnaround. To me the most important thing for Brussels at the moment is to try to leave as much intact as possible until, hopefully, a turnaround. It will have to be triggered by something more radical than anything that has happened during the last years. It must involve something very fundamental and therefore involve economic infrastructure. As far as I know, people are still driving their cars and building their houses. I don't see anything changing.

LDC: That is a circle. There should be a very clear urban policy, a pro-urban policy. Of course, the ideology of the people remains the dream of the cottage and the car. Politicians can see it no other way. They would vote against themselves. Can you compare the situation in Brussels with other cities—New York, for example? Are there strategies to solve these similar problems in New York?

> **RP:** There certainly are generic comparisons to be made, having to do with the changing urban economy and gentrification of cities. But frankly, I haven't seen the situation of Brussels anywhere else. It is quite amazing. You have this combination of investment, hyperdevelopment, and enormous degradation. In my eyes, it doesn't have the same surface logic of American cities and American urban problems. There you have a directed policy for the middle class to leave and a directed policy for containment of the poor. In that entire process you see a pattern. You can logically follow where the change process has happened and why. Here it seems out of control. While there is an interesting patchwork of patterns—as one understands everything to have its own logic—it is hard to decode. In Brussels there is a clear urban culture, much older than anything in the States—all the reminiscences of the High Gothic town, for example. But there is a huge contradiction in that; it is impossible to understand why this spatial and cultural fabric is not fully occupied. In the States it is easier to understand, and in fact the old fabric is becoming reoccupied much faster than it is here.

LDC: Maybe Brussels is an exception in this respect. If you compare Brussels with the capitals of our neighboring countries, Paris and Amsterdam, there is a sort of real and mythical reinvestment in the city.

> **RP:** But of course your neighbors have much larger catchment areas. In Paris, an enormous population outside of the sixteen "arrondissements" is maintaining a relatively small central core. The entire post-war periphery of Paris is responsible for maintaining a relatively small jewel. Here it is different. The balance of urban and rural is more ambiguous because Belgium is a much smaller country. You can't simultaneously maintain the high level of urban centers and have the dispersal, there is just not enough critical mass.

> **VP:** Can you refer to the Brussels situation from a global point of view—that it is a capital city on the national and European scale?

RP: I think that to a certain extent the self-image of Brussels has become warped in the past fifty years. It is a European capital perhaps because of its weaknesses, not because of its strengths. That is why NATO could "invade" it in the first place. It is not an accident that they put their command here, where two cultures remain in conflict—in a place where no one could say "no" and within the context of the Cold War. Advancing from NATO to the capital of the European Community is very easy and logical, based upon the same circumstances.

> **VP:** Maybe this is one of the reasons why Brussels is not working as a city, because it is an artificial capital.

RP: I think that the city is probably not really in control of its destiny. The local politicians are not in control. Brussels was used as a testing ground by global forces. But perhaps this story is not entirely negative. When you consider the city's position, the chaos, and the many aspects of conflict, Brussels actually becomes quite interesting. I think the struggle of the city is in fact a sign of life for the future. Something interesting will surely come out of this.

LDC: What I like is the hybrid quality of Brussels, which in the end could be its source of energy. It is an ultimate thing as opposed to the rather homogenous faces of Paris, Amsterdam, and Antwerp. They might be doomed to become completely "Disneyfied." Bruges was sacrificed a long time ago. Ghent is moving in the same direction. They are beautiful cities, but they have changed into proverbial "theme parks." Their centers are just too good to be true, so "medieval" and in a sense anti-urban. However, it could be that in the end—although it might seem to be a big nostalgic thing coming from some intellectuals—people choose a city because it is a hybrid. The question however remains: is this hybrid quality of Brussels the germination for a possible salvation? Brussels is really a city; it is the only real city we have in Belgium.

> **RP:** I would go with that.

47

LDC: I liked what you just said—the little piece of optimism—if only we could keep things a little as they are, as much as possible, and just wait.

> **RP:** We are too close to a period of enormous urban transformation. We are too close to understand it. Our mentality (from the nineteenth century) of constant destruction, renewal, and addition no longer applies. Western cities are not space-consumptive anymore. They are not growing drastically. From the nineteenth century there [are] enormous areas of unused spatial infrastructure. Urban functions are not consuming space the way cities did some hundred years ago. The danger is that we continue to think in the nineteenth-century manner.

>> **VP:** If you think of strategies in the present debate about Brussels, the accent is on the periphery.

> **RP:** One problem I've had with Open City is that its preoccupation is basically with the center, whereas what is really happening in Brussels is peripheral, in the region. It would seem to have been more effective for Open City to debate the interaction between center and periphery, to contrast them, because they are really one single phenomenon.

LDC: I think Open City should try to make a coherent complete picture of the phenomena it studies. When just focusing on the Canal Zone, or whatever "zone," you can't do the right thing—you don't have a global vision. For Brussels this approach should be obvious: it is the crossroads of all train and car networks for the whole Belgian territory.

> **RP:** Of course what I suggest may be utopian, but given the right political apparatus for control, a lot of the peripheral development could be redirected to those vacant central areas. In fact, much of the peripheral development represents the new space consumptive "industry." Why not place it in the vast unused space at the center, where there is already infrastructure which can be captured and reused? This costs money, of course. It is not as cheap as taking a farmer's field and putting a box on it. But long term it is cheaper. If Brussels had

true planning at the regional level, it would have had to do with redirecting the investment of the periphery towards the center. There are certainly no long-term reasons to not redirect economic development toward the vacant center.

LDC: But the stretch between the Canal Zone and the old center is slowly gentrifying itself. The gentrification is due to private enterprises—involving a kind of micro-investment, with normal people fixing up some blocks. But the city is also investing in some cosmetic interventions—something more sociable for the blocks. These two processes could intertwine and give the area a greater chance of survival. This process is in fact a sort of freezing, but on the positive side it can build something back slowly.

RP: The economics of the situation are such that once the market justifies investment rather than holding for speculation, I think the deadlock will break. In other words, it has to be proven to property owners that investing is more lucrative than waiting. Probably this is starting to happen.

LDC: You said, "there is bound to be some criticism developing against the 'generic.'" The critical context, however, is vanishing. In this age, critical thinking has outlived itself, and that is not only my impression.

RP: Real critical thinking? Reality-based criticism? There is of course "critical theory," which is a different use of the word. I agree with the idea that reality-based criticism is vanishing. But I think this condition is temporary.

LDC: A friend of mine said, "isn't it amazing that in the whole of information technology, which controls basically everything, there is no serious critical thinking?" There is no anti–Bill Gates reading.

RP: No, the critical discourse on information technology happened several years ago, and critical theory about the use of technology more than fifty years ago at the beginnings of the cyber age. It must be in the nature of the technology to silence criticism. Critical discourse aside, I'm sure there will be a popular reaction to the "generic city." How strong it will be is another issue.

49

Perhaps on a mass cultural level it can't happen, but it is happening now in New York, where people are willing to pay full value for a non-generic life, including products, restaurants, specialty stores, etc.

LDC: That might in fact be the only hope for the city: an aesthetic "engagement," a hedonistic commitment.

1 "Evolution of Post-Industrialization and American Urbanism" at the Open City Workshop, Beurs Schouwberg, Brussels, May 11, 1995. Columbia's urban design studios were invited to study development sites in Brussels in collaboration with the Katholieke Universiteit Leuven and the Brussels Open City Program in the spring of 1995, 1997, and 1998, including the areas of the Manhattan Plan and the Thurn und Taxis freight terminals. An architecture studio was also organized in Spring 1996 to study redevelopment of the Cureghem Slaughterhouse area. The following discussion was conducted at the Buersschouwburg in Brussels in Spring 1998, engaging the Belgian philosopher Lieven DeCauter and Véronique Patteeuw, then an editor with NAI Publishers in Amsterdam.

If Not Mostar, Then Where?

Excerpted from "If Not Mostar, Then Where?" in *New Urbanisms: Mostar: Bosnia & Herzegovina* (New York: Columbia University Graduate School of Architecture, Planning, and Preservation, 1998), 6–21; republished in *Mostar 2004 Program, 1994–2004, Final Report*, ed. Amir Pašić (Istanbul: Research Centre for Islamic History, Art and Culture, 2005), 95–99.

Mostar, Stari Most

My first visit to Mostar was in the summer of 1969. I was still a student, caught up in the political currents in the United States—questions of class and race, of de-urbanization, and, of course, of Vietnam. Mostar presented a huge contrast to American society at that moment. There I found an orderly, well-functioning, and integrated urban entity: three religions with all their traditions and symbols coexisting side-by-side. It was a kind of social oasis within the turmoil of global human relations, at least relative to where I was coming from. Even physically the city was a green oasis, nestled in its container of mountains with the prominent symbolism of the sixteenth-century Stari Most—its iconic bridge across the Naretva—still touching to the souls of the late millennium.

My paths crossed several times with Mostar. I was recently moved when I came across the journals of William Stillman (1828–1901), the American painter, photographer, and critic who visited Mostar in 1877. He was amazed by the city: "The city of Mostar is one of the most picturesque I have ever seen."[1] Perhaps this picturesque also pertained to its social structure. By chance, I saw the ABC *Nightline* telecast in New York following November 9, 1992. The Stari Most was down. Like so many others I could not believe my eyes. The symbol of hope that seemed to defy the war had been destroyed. It still seems impossible that Mostar itself could now be in partition, and equally impossible that it might remain this way. A successful reconciliation and reconstruction in Mostar will be of great symbolic and strategic importance in the region. Indeed, as others also have suggested, "If not in Mostar, then where?"

From the perspective of urban design, it is difficult to know where to start with Mostar given the extraordinary destruction of the war and the continuing postwar ethnic partition. The city is also experiencing the pressing "ordinary" problems of an aging post-Soviet and post-industrial city. We began our questioning by taking up where the Soviets left off before the war.[2] We were quickly brought to consider the city as region, the scale at which strategic planning issues in Mostar originate and must be resolved—in much the same manner as any post-Soviet city, regardless of the particulars of the Bosnian context. Mostar as a center of production has disappeared: partly by the destruction of the war and partly through "natural causes."

The invention of new sources of production is essential. Our discourse tended to be dominated by questions of region and of production. As for the highly visible problematic of rebuilding the "historic center," our position was that its future is dependent on the larger context and that the technical problems of immediate reconstruction of monuments were already receiving considerable attention. We therefore started working from the outside in, following the rationale that as goes the region, so goes its *Stari Grad* (Old Town).

That the cessation of industrial production can be attributed to destruction from the war implies that some of this production will revive: the aluminum industry, for example, has again commenced production. The aircraft industry, however, has not. The war heightened the inevitable entropy of the post-Soviet, post-industrial era. The question "what next?" already existed in 1990. Then, as now, the response will be closely related to the new international highway connecting Budapest, through Mostar, to the Adriatic coast. It passes along the eastern edge of the city. The completion of this highway, planned before the war, will be as important to the future of Mostar as the building of the original Stari Most in 1566. The highway will surely have the same power to change the city as countless other roads have changed countless other cities in the second half of this century. The positive side of the Mostar situation is that there is still time to critically plan for this change, unlike countless North American and European counterparts.

At the eastern edge of Mostar, the new international highway will come close to the densest area of the city, up the slope of the mountain where the potential for visual and perceptual pollution will be most extreme. But beyond this most obvious consideration, the planned location of the north and south interchanges for Mostar— removed to the countryside of the ex-urban periphery—would generate large-scale development draining the older city center. This is a commonplace to be avoided at all costs. What is now a relatively compacted urban pattern would elongate along the Naretva River with the interchanges as new centers for investment. Valuable agricultural flatland, which is also important to the aesthetic and economic viability of the city, would be destroyed. The historic center would be affected as well. Until the war, the center supported a diversity of functions in balance with its touristic potential. It is obvious that in the long term, the touristic function of the Stari Grad will reemerge and further evolve, but the question is "in what form?" Can the more fragile non-touristic functions also survive?

This dilemma is intimately connected with the international highway, for which a clear planning strategy is needed. If major investment is made at the periphery, the balance at the center might be lost. The Stari Grad will suffer the same destructive effects of a mono-functional economy based on tourism, as is the case with many other European historic centers. To some extent the potential of the larger "inner periphery" can be reduced as well. In Mostar the formation of the inner periphery was dominated by the logic of Soviet-era urban investment, without the appropriation of density as a function of the marketplace. This fabric requires more investment in order to build a viable urban texture. This opportunity must be met in the context of reconstruction, adding a new layer of growth that responds to new economic realities such that strategic adjustments can be made to the older fabric. This new layer of growth must be added intelligently so as not to destroy the existing city and its historic center.

The Mostar "inner periphery" stretches from the site of the new train station just north of the Stari Grad, through the area of West Mostar, where one will find the dispersed high-rise urbanism of the seventies and eighties. The area of the train station never received enough investment to become a new center for the city. Instead, it has remained open and underbuilt relative to its strategic location. While logically it should become the center of the new city, it remains peripheral. The situation of West Mostar is more ambiguous. It remains an eclectic admixture of high and low building, with villas dating from the Austrian period and high-rise towers from the Soviet era. The fabric is sub-urban in the sense that there is little articulation of street. Of course, it could remain "sub-urban," yet one can understand that the preponderance of available open space, combined with its superior infrastructure and an emerging market economy, could generate considerable pressure for infill and densification. In general, both areas—the station and western sectors—should be allowed to respond to the new market forces. New development on the outer periphery should be held in abeyance for the moment. The danger in locating the interchanges far from the center is that they will stimulate growth at the outer rather than inner periphery. Growth and investment will travel toward the center without ever reaching it. To the contrary, it is the inner city that should generate the investment outward.

The formal characteristics of the city are particularly conducive to the present interregnum of ethnic partition with the Bosniaks on the east side of the Neretva and the Bosnian Croats to the west. More particularly, this divide becomes the "Boulevard" or so-called Front Line near the center of the city, just to the west of and parallel to the Naretva River. The Boulevard has a long history as a line of fracture within Mostar—dating from the time of Austrian governance when it was the line of the railroad tracks that led to the old station. The tracks separated the old city from the new garden extension to the west, which was the province of the Austrians. Under Yugoslav governance, religious ethnic distinctions were relatively sublimated and the Bosniaks were free to integrate the western area of the city. In 1967, with the opening of the new station to the east, the old west side tracks were removed. Their path became the "Boulevard," further reducing the barriers. Yet the void remained in physical reality and in the psyche, easily transformed again into a divide: first as a military "Front Line" in the war and then as an ethnic boundary. The formal logic of the city and its hinterland allowed this fracture to reemerge. Early on in our deliberations it became clear that the Boulevard could be an important starting point, and therefore the preliminary formal analysis was derived from this consideration. The Boulevard had the potential for assimilation into the surrounding fabric, making its former presence almost beyond recognition. Traffic is rerouted and dispersed, and the wide roadway is rebuilt as a local precinct. A series of squares reorganizes the adjoining existing fabric. More than a boulevard, this approach seeks to emphasize diverse connections into the surrounding city and attempts to transform the two "walls" of the old Boulevard into a single structure such that the two sides are one.

The strategy is clear, but like so much else in the continuing struggle of the city, there are multiple readings to be found. One could recognize the positive: an inhabited boulevard instead of a void. One could also envision the negative: a new "wall" instead of a void. The first interpretation evokes a positive symbolism of unity; the second, a negative symbolism of continuing division. Both interpretations surfaced in discussions in Mostar and New York. There is no possibility of knowing for sure how to engage with this question, and for this reason I found this debate to be emblematic of this particular moment in Mostar.

1 William James Stillman, *The Autobiography of a Journalist*, vol. 2 (Boston and New York: Houghton, Mifflin, and Company, 1901), 532.

2 The Spring 1998 Columbia Urban Design Studio was commissioned to work in Mostar on its reconstruction in the context of the collapsed Soviet-era economy and on-going Bosnian War. Field study was conducted in January 2001.

Conversations at the Mezi školami School

Excerpted from "Prague Journal: Conversations at
the Mezi školami School," in *New Urbanisms 5: Prague 13*
(New York: Columbia University Graduate School of
Architecture, Planning, and Preservation, 2000), 13–27.

Prague, Prague 13

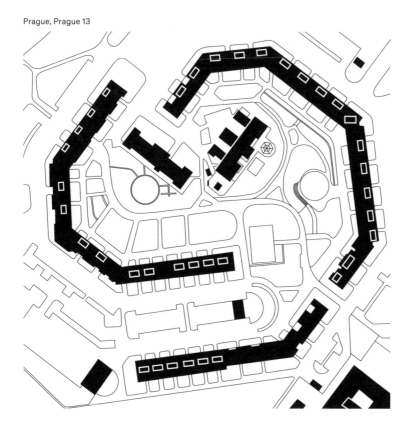

On our first day in Prague 13, we had lunch with Mayor Petr Bratský at the Hotel Franta, where we were staying.[1] It was a quaint old inn, though expanded and modernized, off the little square in Velká Ohrada—the tiny and timeless village adjacent to the *sídliště* (housing development) of the same name, comprising part of Southwest City in Prague 13. Southwest City, with over fifty thousand inhabitants, was the final monument to the communist-era expansion of the City of Prague. Mayor Bratský emphasized that we would hear many views about the state of things, about the problems and opportunities for Prague 13, but that we should be free to make our own judgments and proposals. Afterward, our group spent the afternoon in Prague on a vintage 1939 Praga bus— part of a large collection of Praga vehicles that comprise the new auto museum in Prague 13. The absurd juxtaposition of past and future was lost on nobody as the ancient hulk maneuvered through the old and new city to the considerable confusion of bystanders. An evening reception given by Prague Lord Mayor Jan Kasl reaffirmed the city's official interest in the new ideas that we might bring to the current debate about the future of the city.

The next six days of briefings, discussions, and preliminary studies gave ample evidence of the "many views" mentioned by Mayor Bratský. Our meeting and studio space was located in the elementary school in the Mezi školami in Prague 13, which we shared with about seven hundred schoolchildren—another instructive juxtaposition that provided a constant reminder of the ultimate beneficiaries of our speculations. These six days were extremely well organized, putting on the table, in concise fashion, both the issues and sentiments behind Prague 13 redevelopment, and larger questions of urban and regional development. The most interesting exchanges were related to the dichotomies between the historic center and the Soviet-era vision for a new city, and the divergent natures of the planning instruments needed for each.

The first issue tackled was the advantage of Prague 13's location between two large parks. Second was the question of a proposed new peripheral road and the means to modify its negative effects. Throughout the ensuing days, discussion frequently returned to these two questions, which somehow stereotyped the debate between tendencies toward the "green city" of the communist era and the contemporary Western "city of consumption." The tensions relative to this ideological transposition, the outcome of which no one seemed willing to predict, were very much tied to the question of "master planning." And so it was that the Prague Master Plan—presented by Zdeněk Kovářík, the Prague councilman in charge of city planning—became the first in-depth introduction to planning concepts for the city. Kovářík began by discussing the differences between the Prague model of planning and town planning practice in Great Britain and the United States. He emphasized that the present Master Plan had taken six years to negotiate and approve, and that if a developer presented a scheme for a parcel that did not fit within it, he would have to apply to change it. It was strongly implied that we too should follow the same prudence with whatever we proposed in our studies.

Kovářík outlined the conceptual basis for the Prague Master Plan, stressing the projected structural change in the city from "monocentric" to "polycentric." Because over 50 percent of the present commercial activity in the city was concentrated in the historic core, the polycentric strategy would reduce "stress" on the center through dispersal—one could imagine the enrichment of large residential "estates" from the communist era as a logical outcome. However, the proposed "major new centers" were closer in: Smíchov in Prague 5, the "Manhattan" Pankrác in Prague 4; the nineteenth-century blocks in Karlín in Prague 8; and the abandoned railroad infrastructure in Holešovice in Prague 7. Prague 13, on the other hand, was considered one of a number of "outer centers" beyond these new polycenters.

Hypermarket ("big box") development has been an increasingly dominant feature of the outer centers—controversial because of its negative effects on pre-existent commercial activity. Official policy had not been to stop them, but to "control" them. Ideally, the hyper-sites were allowed at transport exchange points between roads and transit, and one such location would engage Prague 13. Kovářík pointed out that in terms of peripheral development, none of the ring roads were complete, and that topographic features were in fact helping to limit new development, following the logic of the park system. In terms of new development, the Master Plan consisted of "binding" and "nonbinding" conditions. It controlled bulk and density with negotiable variation. Function was also negotiable. Petr Vychodil, deputy director of the ROPID (Regional Planning Authority of Public Transportation System), shed more light on the regional development of Prague 13, emphasizing that there should be more efforts to create jobs in the area and attract higher incomes. Vychodil's main concern was with the relationship between transportation and the emerging regional patterns. While the older monocentric model still dominated, with major job creation still at the center of the city, Vychodil felt that this pattern would change.

Following Kovářík's remarks, several key issues emerged in our discussions. The first being the functional relationship between the Master Plan and the Strategic Plan. Reinforcing

Kovářík, Alena Hořejší of the City Development Authority elaborated on certain details of the Master Plan. She pointed out that the size of the city was projected to increase only slightly from the present-day 1.2 million, a consideration relative to the physical expansion of the city. Hořejší related the city's historical background to its contemporary planning, pointing out that King Charles IV (reign 1346–1378) had devised urban development guidelines that still partially determined building height and bulk. Furthermore, the removal of the fortifications in 1890 significantly altered the morphology of the city. Another major change occurred with the consolidation of Greater Prague in 1922, and then again in 1974, further consolidation established the present boundaries. Impediments to innovation were discussed—from the rigidity of panelized prefab buildings, which comprise almost all of the housing stock, to frozen property titles and property disputes. Hořejší discussed the role of the Master Plan in this chemistry of change, with its designated functions rather difficult to change and its regulations somewhat less so.

Milan Turba, also from the City Development Authority and director of the Strategic Plan, was quick to mention the symptoms of a changing city since communism: the high unemployment level, the steep rise in criminality, and most seriously, the proliferation of private automobile ownership. Automobile use had cut dramatically into mass transit ridership and at least half of the proposed roads for the Prague region were not yet realized. In general, Turba discussed the problems with the monocentric structure of the city, especially relative to the transport sector, and cited the enormous pressure from investors to develop new infrastructure. As for the housing sector, an obvious difficulty resided in the fact that it had not yet been adapted to market principles. Turba also implied that the prediction strategy of the Master Plan was shifting and that a new Master Plan might be needed, even as the most recent plan neared the end of the approval process. From his remarks it was clear that no consensus on the nature of the planning tools needed to manage the Prague situation had been reached. And Turba was careful to distinguish between "public opinion" and "expert opinion" relative to the future direction of the city.

Regarding the question of the post-Soviet lifeworld, Laurent Bazac of CEFRES (French Research Center in Humanities and Social Sciences—Prague) provided a summary of his anthropological studies of Prague 1, which he conducted over several years. He suggested that the "real" Prague—the predominant way of life—existed in the large estates where people live, like Prague 13. The historic center in this constellation, then, was simply a "stage set" relative to the actual life of the city. He noted the physical dislocation between the four old quarters of Prague and the modern city. Diagrammatically, the quarters of the historic center were wrapped by the nineteenth-century belt, separated from the new housing estates by an unbuilt zone. Southwest City was the last estate to be completed in 1982. Built into Southwest City were the sociological consequences of communist-era housing policies. Because of the housing shortage during communism, there were only two ways to get an apartment: have three or four children or find a job that included one. In general, only young couples with children qualified for the new housing. Demographic distinctions were reinforced by sociological distinctions. Those who made it into the estates were people who were successfully working their way up the socioeconomic ladder. They tended not to revisit the old city, where they had lived in poor conditions (many in "fourth category flats" with toilets outside). Relative to where they had come from, Southwest City was perceived to be "ecological," with clean air, nature, no automobiles, and safe areas for children to play outside. The apartments were "first category flats!"

Bazac pointed out that within the constellation of Southwest City, the pre-existent villages remained the most alienated, physically and socially, having very little communication with the new housing. These villages and their particular way of life had existed for centuries; an older woman who was interviewed said that her family had lived continuously in her village since the twelfth century. The superimposition of massive environments of new housing represented a huge trauma for the villagers. No one knew what to call these new forms. According to Bazac, while the architect Ivo Oberstein used the word "superblock," the inhabitants invented the word "rondella." The villagers developed a great anger towards Southwest City, calling the new population "termites." Even after a single generation, social disjunction was still strong, and the isolating force of communism still persisted within the new population of the superblocks. But Bazac argued that counterforces, such as privatization, were tending to change this. Under present laws, for example, cooperatives could emerge—as the new "social contract" became financial.

Bazac was followed by Luděk Sýkora of the Department of Social Geography and Regional Development at Charles University. Sýkora raised the question of whether new businesses in Prague would continue to be located in the historic core. He suggested that the city's chemistry could shift from its communist legacy, and pointed out that the early communists of the Czech Republic were far more interested in an economy based on industrial production than one based on the consumption of housing. However, by the time of the severe housing shortage of the late fifties, the pendulum swung to the opposite extreme. The primary economic activity in Prague engaged housing and it was concentrated at the periphery. By the nineties, after communism, economic activity shifted to the center of Prague, resulting in both the large-scale conversion of the old residential fabric to commercial use and a huge increase in traffic. This hyper-development at the center was supplanted by peripheral office development and new "sub-urban" typologies for retail. Sýkora mentioned the Tesco-IKEA complex and the MAKRO-Luka center, both in western Prague 13, as examples of the latter phenomenon. Because so little was built under communism, there is a pent-up demand for retail space (there is still a very low ratio of square meters per capita). On the other hand, housing production today remains relatively minor compared to what it was and it is oriented toward new wealth in the form of lower-density suburban typologies.

Among other recent phenomena discussed by Sýkora was the shifting demand for nineties office development, from the historic center to "back office" space farther out—cheaper and larger space connected by roads, transit, and communications—a transition made by companies like IBM and Sony. Sýkora also mentioned that while some of the peripheral housing estates were deteriorating, Southwest City, including Prague 13, was experiencing an upward trend and attracting new investment. Its advantages included excellent infrastructure and developable land. Sýkora did not agree with certain dire predictions that claimed housing estates will become ghettos in the long run. In fact, like Bazac, he emphasized that from the beginning, these estates represented the "middle class" of communism and that they could not be easily ghettoized. Indeed, there was no foreseeable housing alternative for the middle class. The single-family house still remained out of reach for most families, and the subsidies required for its mass production were not forthcoming. The estates still hold the key to the city's well-being.

Prague 13's present situation was further elaborated by Iveta Karvaiová of the Prague 13 Municipal Planning Office and a resident of the Southwest City panel housing. She emphasized the advantages of Southwest City—that it is a community with open space, that it is safe for children, and that it is more convenient than the congested urban center. However, Karvaiová argued that there were still not enough public amenities to make it a "city" rather than a "hostel" of bedrooms. There was little reason to spend time there. Southwest City had neither the jobs nor the developed public spaces to draw people. She mentioned how the uniform technology of the panel housing prevented people from adjusting to their homes. There remained the basic challenge of how to create "urbanity," or find the connectiveness to normative systems of the city. And to the far west, at the "West City" area beyond Southwest City, the situation remained very undefined due to the lack of both infrastructure and guidelines. It became more and more apparent that the Master Plan was considered only hypothetical to some, especially for open sites at the periphery.

Professor Martin Matějů of the Department of Cultural Studies of Charles University began his discussion of "panel culture"— mentioning the Czech films, *Panelstory* (1979) by Věra Chytilová and *Space Odyssey II* (1986) by Jan Svěrák. He emphasized the importance of the culture of these estates, which provided housing for one-third of the Czech Republic. Matějů provided an analysis of socialization among the panel dwellers, emphasizing that while the estates did not give enough opportunity for social interaction, social relationships, such as they are, remained friendly. Typically based on blood relationships among families, social relationships within the estates were beginning to open up to other kinds of interaction. One factor in the intensification of the social dynamic was linked with the growing pressure of space constraints. Propinquity within the realm of habitation was increasing, whether people liked it or not. Of course there was a large proportion of "public space" in the estates, but still no public social utilities—the everyday urban amenities usually associated with normal informal socialization—despite the calls for their development. So the socialization remained "primitive," and outside of the rich traditions of Czech urban culture.

Alexandra Brabcová, currently associated with the Open Society Fund Praha, also spoke about socialization. Brabcová was previously staff advisor to the Lord Mayor of Prague, and in this capacity she initiated the Columbia Urban Design Program's involvement in Prague 2000 activities. Brabcová had lived in a housing estate for eighteen years and she hated every minute of it, "not one pleasant memory." She emphasized that no traditional urbanity existed in the estates. When she left, she was in search of the "street." She argued that it is not enough for people in the estates to simply "share their experience." They must share something larger. She concurred that television and media were overly dominant among the panel environments, stating that it was no accident that the dream of the single-family house came from the estates—that the ideal of *Dallas*, as projected into the apartments, was the dominant one. The problem was exacerbated by the low educational level. The estates were not inspirational

63

environments for learning—the Czech Republic was in fact at the "bottom" in terms of the historical and cultural self-knowledge of its youth. Finally, she reminded us of the fact that living in the estates was not a matter of choice. It was not a question of whether the residents "liked" where they lived, but rather whether it was "comfortable" as a guaranteed minimum existence.

Discussion around the "privatization" of the estates, related to possible effects on patterns of socialization, followed—and we were joined by Petr Starčevič, an architect and planner who recently moved his practice to a new privately developed office and residential complex in Southwest City. Starčevič pointed out that the basic organization of the estates was not conducive to privatization, in the sense that privatization naturally occurred in fragments, and there was nothing about the place that easily lent itself to pieces. There were fundamental questions of who pays for water, or for heating and electricity, building to building. And given that the current regulations that governed the co-opting of buildings required a unanimous tenant consensus to proceed, it was extremely unlikely that this requirement could be met in the estates, or anywhere else in the world, for that matter.

In contrast to Brabcová we also heard from Ivo Oberstein, the former chief architect of Southwest City and current professor of the faculty of architecture at the Czech Technical University in Prague. He was only thirty-three years old when he won the competition to design Southwest City in 1968. It was the last of the big communist estates. During the ceremony there were Soviet tanks in the street below. Because it was built after the Soviet invasion, there was little space for a creative architectural approach. He mentioned having seen projects at the time in France that seemed much better than the Czech estates. Certain goals and ambitions within the project were hard-fought. The designers struggled to save the old villages from the dominant economic ideology— pockets of poverty within a dynamic and modern housing estate.

Oberstein discussed some of the positive aspects of planning Southwest City, including his effort to diversify the housing types. Along with his wife, Oberstein designed the only divergence from the panel buildings: a row of single-family houses along the Ovčí Hájek in Nové Butovice. He fought to humanize the panel system, even in the most minor ways like varying the color of the concrete aggregate. He noted that the rigidity of the panel system was more obvious now in the current democratic climate that valued the home as a site for self-expression. He stated that no more high-rises should be built, only "garden city" typologies. But, compared to social housing in other cities, Oberstein felt Southwest City satisfied its purpose reasonably well.

Discussion included the longevity of the panel buildings. While the panels themselves were welded together, with little flexibility for replacement or removal, people had managed, ingeniously, to cut through them in order to connect to adjacent spaces. Oberstein mentioned ideas about adding a layer of rooms and façades at the slab exteriors. One was left with the impression that the panel buildings could evolve substantially if ownership constraints were overcome. Discussion also included the large increase in automobile ownership in the past decade and its effect on the original Southwest City planning. The original design took into account three and a half inhabitants per vehicle. Today there are two inhabitants per vehicle in Southwest City, which is comparable to Vienna. In the original plan, parking lots were to be converted to garage structures, but few were ever built. Now these garages are rented, and poorer families cannot afford them. According to Oberstein, the popularity of the automobile and the lifestyle around it went hand in hand with that of the single-family house, even though it was very unlikely that the economy would engage this arena of production for the middle class.

At the conclusion of our six-day discussion, we prepared to leave for the ancient towns of South Bohemia: Kutná Hora, Telč, Slavonice, Český Krumlov, and Tábor. Seeing the extraordinary urban constructs within these towns placed the previous days in critical perspective: how much has been lost over the centuries or how much potential is there for the integration of a new urbanism within one of the more intact city centers in Eastern Europe?

1 The Spring 2000 Columbia Urban Design Studio was commissioned to study reconfiguration of the Soviet-era urbanism in the Prague 13 sector. Field study was conducted in January 2000 including an initial session with the Lord Mayor followed by extensive official and other briefings.

Time Capsule

Excerpted from "Time Capsule," in *New Urbanisms 6: Litoral Central, Venezuela* (New York: Columbia University Graduate School of Architecture, Planning, and Preservation with Princeton Architectural Press, 2005), 14–19.

Caracas, 23 de Enero District

During several days in mid-December 1999, the northern face of the Avila Mountain that separates Caracas from the Caribbean received an enormous amount of rainfall. By some estimates, this phenomenon was likely to occur just once every eight thousand years. The extraordinary amount of water precipitated a major natural disaster that was well documented by the global media. The El Litoral coastline was transformed beyond recognition and several towns were effectively erased. By the time of our first post-disaster visit in September 2000, after a period of nine months, basic services and infrastructure had not been restored.[1] By our second visit in January 2001, reconstruction progress was still minimal. No clear consensus existed on a reconstruction strategy. Within this context of uncertainty, our work considered both the toll of the natural disaster and the reconstruction questions it continued to pose. In some locations the disaster unleashed such long-term geologic instability that the issue of rebuilding involved no reasonable answers—not to mention the parallel political instability that many Caraqueños quickly point out that the Avila disaster seems to have presaged.

The metropolitan area of Caracas comprises a population variously estimated up to five million, primarily settled in the inland valley behind the Avila. Throughout most of its history, since its founding by the Spanish in 1567, the importance of Caracas remained primarily regional. Only in the mid-twentieth century did Venezuela's oil production propel the city to global status. The relationship of Caracas to its littoral coast is complicated. The Spanish sited Caracas inland at a high elevation (1,000 meters) for advantages of climate and security. The littoral coast has always been crucial to the city, providing the infrastructure of port, airport, and now cyberport. At the same time, it has always remained estranged, recently becoming part of the Estado Vargas, which is governmentally separate from Caracas—extending the historic dialectic between physical dislocation and cultural integration. Especially on the weekends, El Litoral has functioned as a kind of "Coney Island," a populist urban extension growing from a year-round population of 450,000 to 1.5 million on weekends. El Litoral is sometimes referred to as a social "pressure valve."

More integrated with the city is the Avila landscape, which also enters into the mythology of the city. The Avila provides the most significant physical identity for the city, giving coherence to the modern landscape of towers and barrios. It functions more to unite than to divide the city from its seacoast. All this to say that, among other things, the reconstruction of the coast is of deep "spiritual" significance to Caraqueño identity. But the Avila is also a physical barrier. In spite of the importance of El Litoral to the culture of Caracas, it has never been well connected, separated as it is by the Avila topography. Perhaps psychologically this distance was positive—the existence of another world so near yet so far. In recent history, however, this estrangement has become increasingly problematic, as there is only one route between the city and its airport, seaport, and beaches beyond. And after the Avila disaster this dislocation became a crucial issue relative to strategizing reinvestment. The catch is that the level of investment needed to "restore" the coast could be justified only through inclusion of major new infrastructure to address the hope of providing sufficient social and economic returns. Otherwise, things would stay as they presently are. There has been little public discussion of the stagnation option, though perhaps now, two years later, this too will change in tandem with national politics.

The project addressed how, where, and when to most effectively allocate new infrastructural investment relative to an overall future vision for El Litoral. There are basic large-scale alternatives, for example, involving a highspeed road and/or rail corridor, a new tunnel providing a loop to the eastern area of Caracas, and new airport and seaport infrastructure at the western area of the coast—projects long in the arena of public discussion. Throughout our studies, these options gradually disappeared from our scrutiny. Our attention instead shifted to less expensive and more flexibly integrated strategies. In this regard, it is important to note our diffidence in portending a continuity with the vast Venezuelan modernist project for Caracas, given its obvious limitations in hindsight. And it was equally difficult to follow a strict adherence to orthodox modem developmental ideals in a city that is well over half "illegitimate" relative to orthodox developmental criteria. The idea evolved to "leapfrog" the hegemony of modernism to another level.

Such was our aversion to large mono-functional infrastructure and, instead, our predisposition toward the flexibilities that accompany a more cumulative approach. The idea of the developmental catalyst or "trigger" became central to each intervention proposal. Developmental "packages" surfaced for which conditional mechanisms could be predicted in substitution of traditional linear investment progressions, such that individual pieces may or may not happen without threatening whole outcomes. This approach would begin with a generalized site exploration— *ad hoc* groundwork comprised of a survey of comprehensive site potentials—and then develop into more dedicated particular programmatic/locational strategies. First, it involved the limits of a discourse and then a core discourse. At the heart of this dialogue was the identification of a potential array of "triggers" with

69

investigation of the likely developmental potentials and imped-
ances associated with each. Several involved a certain faith in new
urban economic generators as fallout from globalization and its
positive localized effects.

A companion to this discourse was the continuing relevance
of two extraordinary briefing sessions in Caracas, which put firm-
ly in evidence the complexities surrounding the El Litoral reconstruction, both political and tectonic—not to mention studio
reviews in New York that highlighted the fluidity of outlooks
among students and guests. A major point of contention involved
approaches to infrastructural investment. For example, from the
beginning, the architect and urbanist Carlos Gómez de Llarena
insisted that the completion of the long-proposed modern coastal
highway project—an urban "corniche" looped back into Caracas
through a tunnel under the Avila—be a priority. This project
was easily dismissed by many students as far too costly given
the current realities of the Venezuelan political economy. Yet,
notably, the majority of the final proposals were obliged to admit
to the necessity of this option toward realizing a reasonable
regional movement infrastructure. At the opposite end of the
spectrum, the microscale proponents also had their voice in the
students' thinking. One such voice belonged to the anthropolo-
gist Patricia Márquez, whose studies of new forms of microenter-
prise were particularly useful. Márquez makes intriguing connections between new telecommunications infrastructure, which is
certainly global and expansive, and the critical importance of cell
phones to new informal sector microbusiness—its liberating
effect on women who have become crucial in this new entrepre-
neurial class.[2]

Now, after two more years, nothing expansive has happened
in El Litoral relative to reconstruction, although there is no question that much has changed politically both in Venezuela and in
the world. One could argue that our work represents a naive idealism that no longer applies. But it is also true, perhaps now more
than ever, that this idealism is important to keep alive. Or at least
one can argue it is an idealism that sooner or later must resurface.
In many ways this project represents a form of "time capsule" such
that it will be here when the discourse reemerges. At the end of the
day, our function has been to keep alternatives on the table.

1 The Spring 2001 Columbia Urban Design Studio was commissioned to plan strategies for reconstruction following the Avila disaster. Field studies were conducted in September 2000 and January
2001 confronting the large loss of life and infrastructure. A previous studio in Spring 1997 had
studied informal fabric adjoining the Cota Mil.
2 Márquez's work on the informal sector was subsequently published as *Socially Inclusive Business:
Engaging the Poor Through Market Initiatives in Iberoamerica* (Cambridge, MA: Harvard University
Press, 2010).

After Shopping

Excerpted from "After Shopping—What We Did," in *After Shopping. Situation Salzburg—Strategies for the Speckgürtel,* ed. Eva Held, Norbert Mayr, Richard Plunz and Barbara Wally (Salzburg: Verlag Anton Pustet, 2003), 9–15.

Salzburg, Europark 2, Taxham

In Salzburg, to the east, the festival was already underway, but although even the most distant Alpine Valleys, beyond the passes, tunnels, gorges, even borders, felt its reverberations, Taxham, right nearby, remained untouched ...

— Peter Handke, *On a Dark Night I Left My Silent House*[1]

At hand was the task of understanding the Speckgürtel phenomenon in Salzburg. We hoped to probe beyond the Salzburg Festival and the mythic city—to exactly what was happening in the "real" Salzburg, at Taxham and elsewhere, peripheral places untouched by the branding of Festival and Mozart.[2]

Our probe began with the Salzburg of the periphery, the Salzburg where the new money moves. We were interested in the idea that the city was more than Festival. We noted that the July 2000 issue of *Wired* magazine showed Salzburg at the edge of one of the most important hubs of information delivery in the world. Surely this strategic position could mean something? Then there was the question of the recent removal of European borders—the hypothetical unification with the neighboring South Bavarian cultural and economic landscape. Could even Hitler's old bastion at Berchtesgaden now be seen within a seamless suburban extension of Salzburg rather than Munich? Then there was the Speckgürtel itself, which was an initial fixation. Is this peripheral ring or "belt of fat" a positive appellation that signifies the power of the Salzburg economy? Or is it a derogatory epithet signifying a parasitic drain on the inner city? We assumed that understanding the Speckgürtel phenomenon was key to understanding the Salzburg "situation." Certainly this hunch gained in credibility at the symposium on the Speckgürtel in collaboration with our *Salzburger Nachrichten*. This exercise in *realpolitik* gave the overwhelming impression of an intriguing game of "cat and mouse" around questions of the Salzburg periphery and regional unity.

A conceptual starting point was Taxham, from Peter Handke's novel *On a Dark Night I Left My Silent House* (2000), which tells the story of an unnamed pharmacist's hallucinatory journey from the suburb. Through his perceptions we found our stride, and a certain infectious irony and humor. Handke's Taxham is everywhere and nowhere—it is emblematic of the generic and global, and of the interchangeability of location and culture. When Handke's protagonist sees his vision of Taxham in Spain, he is moved to ask if he "ever left the City of Salzburg?" Could Taxham function as a potent symbol of all that the periphery must be—or must not be?[3] For Handke, it is a "clearing in the airport forest."[4] For politicians, it is triumphant with its landmark Europark shopping mall, Portzamparc's high-style exercise in global genericism and breakthrough innovation (parking on the roof). Beginning with Taxham, we traversed Handke's circuitous path from the "New Old City" of Salzburg to around the globe.

Our narrative followed the trajectory of the Speckgürtel from south to north. We started from the A-10 interchange below Anif—where there is a proposal to augment the new suburban domestic cottage enclaves with a new suburban university at the Urstein-Au brownfield; then to the area north of Wals-Siezenheim, an area marked by hyper-development at its most amoebic state; to Taxham and the area of the Klessheim Castle and its Baroque garden, now dominated by massive parking and a proposed new stadium for Salzburg; to the malls of the Airport Center and the Europark precedent; and onward toward the north and the bifurcated town of Liefering; and to Eugendorf with its accumulation of "big boxes." The Salzburg mythologies of Mozartkugeln are amply contrasted by the realities of the Speckgürtel, including the denial of Speckgürtel presence by local high culture. But the Speckgürtel is not seen as entirely negative. In these contradictions we found a certain parallel in the Mozartkugel phenomenon—it too denies historical reality. Mozart actually disliked Salzburg immensely.

Our work involved questions of continuity, the issue of present-day hyper-development relative to historical patterns and to sublimation—whether or not there was "always a periphery." We worried that our fledgling critiques were too alarmist. What are possible similarities between history and now? Could the world of Mozart still reign as some form of "reality?" We pursued this line of analytic protocol, but found little supporting evidence for continuity beyond the superficialities of "theme park."

Our primary historical interest engaged the evolution of infrastructure relative to urban densification. The river, roads, railroads, autobahn, and fiber-optic net were examined relative to historical continuity. The older infrastructure had transformed, but the newer infrastructure now transforms it all, including the older infrastructure. The river, once a regional lifeline, had become decorative. The reaches of the local railroads contracted, although there are now hopes to re-establish its viability. The historic road typologies were eclipsed by the autobahns, which also eclipsed the function of the railroads while extending the built fabric to more distant peripheries. And the latest layer of infrastructure, the fiber-optic net, has yet to fully expose its full significance and effect. Perhaps cyberspace could counter the ever-expanding peripheral urban sprawl through a logic of proxemics.

We imagined the "Outer Periphery" as an urban landscape, with mechanisms of urbanization that appear to govern its future. It was noted that the catchment area of Salzburg as an urban entity regionalized, pushing even farther into the cheap and abundant land outside old municipal boundaries. At the same time, the cachet of "Old Salzburg" continues to be exploited at an ever-greater distance. For Salzburg to maintain this cachet, however, it must protect its remaining open land at all costs, and suffer the opportunistic land consumption of its neighboring municipalities. Salzburg's decision to preserve open space came rather late in the game—the remaining open land had lost much of its coherence. The historical logic of agriculture and small village settlements at the edge of the old city has been replaced with another logic. All that remains of the open space is marginalized into residual parcels. The open space dilemma says a lot about the importance of regional development controls to the future of the "Old City" and vice versa.

While Salzburg has reserved 58 percent of its territory as "green space," 50 percent of the remaining buildable open land is single-family houses. Salzburg is choking on its own low-density growth. At the same time, the dense historic center is underused. Its inhabitants have decreased drastically in recent times, from twelve thousand in 1890 to four thousand today. The proliferation of the iconic single-family house is both dream and reality, yet its efficiency can hardly be seen as a long-term sustainable condition because of its saturation of the land availability. Local testing of low-rise, high-density prototypes is important to both the rural and urban futures. "Inner Periphery" sites are strategic in this densification. We realized that the Inner Periphery was more strategic to our understanding of "Situation Salzburg" than the Speckgürtel. It is strategic for the redensification of the region, in terms of both building and cultural activity. For us, nurturing a "new culture" could be a critical component of renewal, which pointed toward the importance of official support for the existing initiatives in this realm. We were surprised to discover a certain vibrancy of new culture in a city so marked by public branding rooted in historicist culture.

The issue of "shopping" existed from the beginning, both because of its dominance as an economic engine at the periphery and for its obvious decline at the center—hastened by the decline in the Old City population and the increase in tourism. Although we were careful to note that the new generic shopping economy seems to thrive in the Salzburg metropolitan area overall, much older localized shopping has been destroyed—with an Old City ghettoized by tourists and devoid of residents, and an Inner Periphery of abandoned shops, lost to an Outer Periphery of malls. Thus, beyond positive shopping revenues overall, Salzburg as the "City of Shopping" has its problems, which a comparison between Europark and Alt Stadt made clear enough. Are they really "much the same," or does the Old City simply provide the scenography for the peripheral malls where the real business is?

So we departed from Handke. Even Taxham has been touched! The limits of the branding of the city were obvious: "After Shopping" came to entail a fragile discourse including "After Mozart!" Salzburg as Generic City must be resisted, but the form of the resistance was not obvious given the the advanced state of the city's branding. Would a "Shopping-Free Zone" represent a form of cultural resistance or simply be another marketing strategy? This consideration led to the ultimate question—a question raised by Naomi Klein, whose *No Logo* (1999) helped focus our final work. The question involves the conflicted position that much cultural critique suffers at this moment—the individual dilemmas of survival beyond the cynicism of critical abstraction on one hand and the cynicism of participation on the other. Klein is critical of the "in-between" or "ironic consumption," of playing both sides. Perhaps in this aspect of our questioning, we could find no better insight than the insight offered by Klein.[5] But our work on the "Situation Salzburg" gave these issues a degree of reality and immediacy—a "moment of truth," which was lost on none of us.

1 Peter Handke, *On a Dark Night I Left My Silent House* (New York: Farrar, Straus & Giroux, 2000), 14.
2 Reference is made to the masterclass at the Salzburg Summer Academy taught by the author and Hubert Klumpner in 2001 and focused on the Salzburg periphery. The author also taught a previous masterclass in 1998.
3 Handke, *On a Dark Night I Left My Silent House*, 161.
4 Ibid.
5 Naomi Klein, *No Logo. Taking Aim at the Brand Bullies* (New York: Picador, 1999), 78–83.

Notes from along the Val di Cecina

Excerpted from "Setting the Stage: Notes from along the Val di Cecina," in *New Urbanisms 7: Geothermal Larderello: Tuscany, Italy* (New York: Columbia University Graduate School of Architecture, Planning, and Preservation, 2005), 35–53.

Larderello, Enel Centrale 3

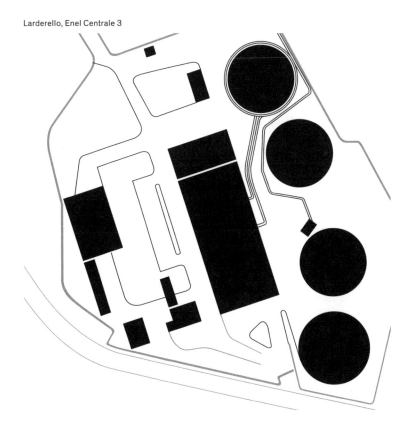

As soon as we arrived in Rome it was clear that the scope of our study would not begin or end with the future of several geothermal sites in Tuscany.[1] The originator of the project, Paolo Pietrogrande, then still the CEO of Enel Green Power, immediately took our group to the Montemartini Museum. Originally the site of the first electric generation plant in Rome, the building had recently been restored. The machine hall, with its enormous diesel engines, now held four hundred sculptures from the Capitoline Museums, organized in three periods related to the evolution of the ancient city. Pietrogrande would have us understand that ancient culture, modern science, and urban development are interrelated in a powerful admixture that might be the starting point for our mandate. In my mind, his passion for engineering as a cultural enterprise had a certain resonance with the Futurism of Antonio Sant'Elia, and other Italians at the turn of the twentieth century that engaged engineering as a multilayered and transformative force deep within our culture, with profound connections to urbanism.

During our first day at Larderello we were introduced to a number of locations along the southern section of the Val di Cecina. We had our first views of the Valle del Diavolo ("Valley of the Devil"), renowned for centuries for its great plumes of steam, which, at least in the folkloristic accounts, had influenced Dante and become his inspiration for *Inferno*. Enel's geothermal electric generation facilities at Larderello represent an extraordinarily diverse range of extant conditions and issues—including the abandoned monumental 1950s power plant Number 3, with its great gravity-fed cooling towers, in contrast to the relatively recent, certainly less imposing and equally less interesting, Valle del Secolo plant designed by Aldo Rossi, with its state-of-the-art mechanical cooling system. Throughout the trip, Pierdomenico Burgassi, the former director of the Enel facilities at Larderello, was a limitless resource of historical and technical information, his family having a long involvement with the area over many generations. Perhaps for this reason, Burgassi was quick to point out a socio-technological conundrum underlying our presence there. In the 1950s, when the plant Number 3 was constructed, perhaps seventy-five workers would be needed to control the system; now, the same tasks are automated with only a few persons.

Certainly the cooling towers and the networks of the bright metallic steam pipes provide an impression of engineering monumentality on the scale of Sant'Elia. The towers, remarkable eight to ten-story objects in the landscape with unimaginable interior spaces typically never seen by the public, fascinated us—and it turned out that they also hold a great fascination for many of the local population. Rather than "industrial blight" on the rolling landscape of medieval villages and farms, these more recent additions are seen as improvements on the previous layers—proud symbols of an important livelihood that offer the intrigue of a modern Dantean landscape. At one of our stopping points, Monterotondo Marittimo at the southernmost end of the valley, the old hilltop fabric and nearby modern cooling tower seemed entirely complementary.

At Monterotondo, a local historian named Lara Pippucci recited his passionate knowledge of a millennium of local history, and not before too long arrived at the question of the future of the past—a question which came to dominate discussions everywhere. From the Etruscans came the basic infrastructure and settlement pattern reinforced and sublimated over the centuries, including the hot springs at Bagnone near Sasso Pisano—a large and important center in the pre-Roman world, now under excavation. The site has its devotees like archaeologist Clara Ghirlandini, who described efforts to reinforce the importance of it today. Not far away, another geothermal site called Lagoni Rossi—now where a church and a few houses from the last century sit abandoned—also posed the question of the future. Then there was Serrazzano, the medieval hill town on a Roman site, semi-abandoned until recently—evidence of a first wave of reoccupation worth noting, a gentrification in part attributed to its location just forty minutes from the seashore.

Very interesting were the formal briefings in the auditorium of the Museo della Geotermia di Larderello (Geothermal Museum). Paolo Pietrogrande's introduction began with the cautionary note that technology had its many layers even in Larderello, and that its real origins involved the "chemistry business" traced back to the Etruscans—with power generation coming rather late in 1904. The cultural offspring of geothermal activity reaches recent times, not the least of which is Giovanni Michelucci's modernist Larderello "new town" of the 1950s, with his masterpiece Parish Church. Now it is half-empty and clearly symbolizes the transition from the era of labor-intensive electric production to today's high degree of automation.

The economist Federico Simoncini, affiliated with the principal regional bank Cassa di Risparmio di Volterra, further elaborated on the "stagnation" question, emphasizing that for Tuscany "beauty is not enough." For Simoncini, the bright spots in the economic landscape are industry and fashion in the Arno Valley, textiles in Prada, and heavy machinery in several locations. Yet all enterprise faces a difficult moment. In the Val di Cecina, apart from Enel, the main industries are tourism and craft production, primarily related to alabaster. And Simoncini explained that from the 1970s onward, demand for alabaster has continually dropped. The industry underwent a restructuring toward mass production to accommodate a surge in large orders, but this demand slacked off and the industry was left with mass production techniques and no market. Meanwhile, the "artisanal content" was lost, which was the attraction of alabaster in the first place. Simoncini emphasized that it will take a long time to recover what was lost, engaging a "new way" of small scale and quality.

Simoncini likewise emphasized the general economic fragility of the region, especially with the projected growth rate of only one-half of the nation's average. And while the local real estate market shows potential, Simoncini viewed real estate as a kind of "refuge," not capable of "commodification." For example, he basically argued that his bank, the Cassa di Risparmio di Volterra, feels the need to invest in "something new" other than real estate, and this need has led to a certain interest in the "renewable energy business." That said, the Larderello area continues to develop as a real estate market. The European Community influence has been important in this development, nurturing the "country house" phenomenon and the agritourism industry that is still evolving.

We then heard from Gabriele Simoncini, the director of a new branch of the International School of Graduate Studies in Pisa with a new building in Volterra. Simoncini connected this project to the need for a "new cultural presence," and "new players," in the area. He argued that while the area has a lot to offer, there is a lack of ideas about how to develop its resources. A "new mentality" is needed to move beyond the time of the Renaissance, which in his view is where most minds still reside. Simoncini argued the growing importance of globalization in education as a cultural (and economic) generator. He emphasized that if the university is where knowledge is transferred, it must now be transferred globally—a broad spectrum of sources between many universities, not just bilateral agreements between two. He pointed to the importance of "niche universities" in this new formulation—that is, specific micro-scale institutions with global connections.

Gabriele Simoncini was followed by Patrizia Pietrogrande, an architect in Florence who presides over an innovative company for the development and marketing of environmental projects. Pietrogrande's firm had made a proposal for tourist development at Larderello, which focused on identifying why people might be interested in this isolated area and how they could be motivated to visit. Her study found big potentials in certain aspects of the natural geothermal activity, for example, the possible development of new thermal bath sites. Pietrogrande was also very interested in the visual landscape of the large cooling towers and their potentials for reuse. She related some of her previous experience with redevelopment of older industrial locations, most importantly the Ducati Factory in Bologna. For the Ducati project, she was presented with a functioning factory, but a phase of outsourcing and noncore production. Her presentation extended the discussion about handcraft and global exposure. A museum was built within the factory, in part as a marketing tool. Integral to the museum was the present-day production line. Visitors are exposed to a view of the product normally invisible to the public—they become associated with the product through education. Not inconsequently, in this strategy, visitors are motivated to buy a Ducati, and can even arrange to follow the production of their own machine. Pietrogrande described other innovative projects in Florence, such as a strategic plan to increase tourism in the winter. This program involved the collective organization of smaller museums and other cultural institutions as an "alternative city" for visitors already familiar with the major cultural attractions.

Next came Gabriella Belli, an architect with the Sovrintendenza di Monumenti di Pisa, which has jurisdiction over the Val di Cecina. After describing how this local jurisdiction works, Belli discussed the intriguing question of what a "monument" is, and about broadening such definitions. In this context, the cooling towers again came up as "modern monuments" in the landscape. She described how the Comune di Monterotondo had requested the preservation of one of its cooling towers and how, as a result, it remains in production. A similar line of thinking came from Francesca Balestrieri, who had recently completed an urban plan for the Larderello area for her thesis at the Università La Sapienza in Rome. Her thesis called for giving "new life to the land of tubes." She was referring, of course, to the complex web of silver pipes emanating from the geothermal steam sources and crisscrossing the landscape to feed the electric generating stations. Like the cooling towers, this relatively recent technological layer on the timeless landscape was seen as a source of great aesthetic interest.

Briefings continued at the palazzo of the Communità Montana in Pomarance, beginning with more specific planning issues related to roads and transport. By now the local population's very high level of dissatisfaction with road infrastructure was clear. The discussion began, however, with the outsider view of architect Edoardo Zanchini from Rome, director of the Italian national environmental group Legambiente. He discussed his organization's interest in new development models, especially pertaining to the kind of landscape issues that exist around Larderello. He emphasized that the problem was not just a matter of modernizing through road building—that, in fact, there is no money for such new heavy road infrastructure, especially prohibitive in the region because of difficult local topography. He also pointed to the high cost of simply maintaining what already exists. Should new roads somehow be built, Zanchini argued that they would transform the area in a negative way—toward "extensive" rather than "intensive" tourism. Zanchini elaborated on some of the questions raised by proposals for new road infrastructure, beginning with the general point that the Italian landscape is an extremely valuable part of the national patrimony, and that much of it has already been destroyed, especially due to the big infrastructure projects after World War II. He added that any additional infrastructural investment must be prioritized, and the importance of public transport should be paramount. Perhaps most importantly, Zanchini questioned the canonical modern idea that new highways are needed to connect places that are isolated in order to promote their development. Instead he argued that the opposite is the case, and that there has been no big investment in new road infrastructure in Italy for the past twenty years.

One growth industry in the Val di Cecina has been "agritourism," and this was described by Andrea Cinotti of the Communità Montana, an association of the local municipalities including Castelnuovo, Monte Verde, Pomarance, Montecatini, and Volterra, with representatives elected by each community. For the past decade or more, the national government has subsidized local tourist initiatives based on agriculture. Thus far, in the Val di Cecina, half of the funds went to environmental improvement such as organic farming, a quarter went to specific farm improvement, and a quarter to tourism development. Discussion included the possible advantages for agritourism, and other such new industry in the region as a consequence of cheaper geothermal energy. Roberto Parri, an engineer with Enel Green Power, enumerated the elements of geothermal infrastructure in place: thirty electric generator plants, four hundred steam wells, four hundred kilometers of pipe to transport the steam to the generator plants, and a total of six-hundred-megawatt electric production—all of this producing energy at a cost lower than conventional fuels, including their subsidies. Parri pointed to the fact that due to inefficiencies, presently only 20 percent of the steam within the system is put to use. The rest is wasted. Were it better recuperated, the energy would be even cheaper. Massimo Rossetti, director of "Parvus Flos," raised the interesting point that perhaps the future use of steam may relate more efficiently to direct thermal application rather than electric production. Parvus Flos, a local business organization for disabled persons, which runs greenhouses at Radicondoli, currently employs thirteen persons. Their production includes flowers and basil (a thousand plants per day on average).

A series of "mobile briefings" were held along the northern end of the Val di Cecina, beginning with an introduction to the new geothermal domestic heating plant for Pomarance constructed by Orion S.C.R.L. It was explained in detail by engineers Fiorenzo Borelli of Orion and Rodolfo Marconcini of Enel Green Power. The valley could enjoy significant economic advantage if advanced technology was applied universally to geothermal heating. The only limit was the need for close proximity to the source in order to avoid excessive condensation—meaning that the steam could not be "exported" over long distances and that the valley could not be consolidated around this energy system. In contrast to this was the ancient technological landmark, the Carporciano copper mine at Montecatini, said to be the "oldest copper mine in Europe," in continuous production until 1907. With its vast underground tunnel system and early industrial processing facility, the copper mine is now a large archaeological site being excavated and stabilized for tourism purposes. Augusto Mugellini, the supervising engineer responsible for this work, was careful to emphasize the relationship between these industrial-era ruins and the new cultural activities envisioned for the site. The lofty old hill town itself was already well gentrified. Over an informal lunch discussion, Mayor Renzo Rossi seemed well-informed about strategies for new cultural production and a new economy for the town. And indeed, here perhaps more than anywhere else in the Val di Cecina, one could sense some real momentum and sophistication in nurturing this approach.

In Volterra, we found ourselves surrounded by the extraordinary evidence of Etruscan culture represented at the Guarnacci Etruscan Museum. Museum director Gabriele Cateni made a point of emphasizing the continuities of history—in this case reaching back more than three millennia—and the importance of the vagaries of daily existence then and now. Present-day dilemmas were evident during our subsequent visit to the Rossi alabaster factory, where the degeneration of this ancient art form was clear—now as objects for tourism rather than ceremony. Historical contrasts were emphasized even more at Poggibonsi, near Florence, where we gathered in the Castello della Magione dell'Ordine dei Cavalieri del Tempio—an organization and building dating to the Crusades of the fourteenth century. We met with Tommaso Franci, *Assessore* for the environment for the region of Tuscany. The complexities in the diversity of our relatively small geographic area, and the limits of political economy operating at all scales from global to hamlet, became clear in this meeting. Franci was able to describe several innovative projects in Tuscany that involved technology, environment, and culture and that could point toward possible directions for our work.

At the Palazzo Vecchio in Florence, we heard firsthand from Francesco Colona, *Assessore* for trade and production, about the limits of a tourism-based economy. We heard once again about the importance of an "engaged" touristic economy in order to avoid the pitfalls of "mass" tourism and the difficult Florentine situation involving millions of short-term tourists every year (Zancini's "extensive tourism") that cost more to "clean-up" than the euros they spend, at least as far as municipal income is concerned. The question arose as to what might be alternatives, apart from agritourism? Several ideas were discussed, some related to the refitting of old production sites: the salt mine and production plants at "Salina," the hydrochloric acid production plants at Saline, and the boric acid production plants at Larderello. Other initiatives were mentioned by Armando Burgassi of Co.Svi.G., including the fish farm at Castelnuovo, which uses geothermal energy to maintain water temperatures. Burgassi also mentioned initiatives involving the end products of milk production (ricotta cheese) and end products of the wood industry (composite materials made from bark or even cornstalks).

These intense days of briefings and the immersion in the realities of Larderello and the Val di Cecina formed the "program" to be followed by our team—explored in a very preliminary way at the Villa Ginori in Castelnuovo and synthesized as strategic options presented to an audience that included those who had previously briefed us. These discussions had considerable influence on our subsequent work and served to prove that indeed "reality is stranger than fiction"—or at least as interesting. The stage was set for our work, and months later, these conversations along the Val di Cecina remained at the heart of our ideas.

1 The Spring 2003 Columbia Urban Design Studio was commissioned to study the redevelopment of geo-thermal sites in Larderello in Tuscany. Field study was conducted in January 2001 entailing extensive briefings organized by Enel Green Power, the owner of the sites.

Talking of the Han River

Excerpted from Richard Plunz and Byoung-soo Cho,
"Dialogue: Talk about the Han River," *Space* (2007): 102–103.

Seoul, Seun Sangga

Richard Plunz: How do you as an architect from Seoul feel about the future of Seoul? When I was there last year with Columbia students, I developed both an enormous enthusiasm for what I saw and a discomfort about what might come next—decisions to be made and the capacity of the design field to make a difference in those decisions. How does the future play out in your mind? In terms of urban design, can Seoul be in 2020 what Barcelona was in 1990? Certainly the Han River restoration is a start?[1]

Byoung-soo Cho: Yes, it has been a one-way process from East to West. In the future, I think things, in terms of overall systems, systems of operation, and systems of value, will continue this way, fortunately and unfortunately. But within the systems, there is certainly going to be a stronger impact from the West. The impact will be felt in a positive way based on the different perspectives or attitudes that still exist in the society and culture of Korea, Japan, and China. These impacts could potentially be as strong as the ones we had in the Expressionist and modernist movements, through Cezanne, Manet, Monet, Van Gogh, and Mondrian; as well as Frank Lloyd Wright and R. M. Schindler. And they could contribute again to the directional flow of culture, especially in art and architecture, and on a spiritual level. Certainly the impact could be given much greater velocity than before due to the greater speed and volume of global exchange today and in the future.

As an architect, I feel pain about Seoul and its future. Political systems and politicians, such as the mayor and district directors, have all the decision-making powers in Korea, and often the decisions are made based on persuasive political directions and shortsighted popularity. Sometimes they make good decisions, but more often they choose bad decisions, even though they are smart. Some try to relate the projects under development to the election and term itself.

For example, the Han River project has suddenly become a very hot issue for everybody in Seoul since the candidates of Seoul City talked about it last year. Mayor Lee (Myung-bak) announced that we are going to have a performing arts center on a small island on the Han River, without any concern for the bigger picture or long-term plan. If it continues this way, I am pessimistic about the future of Seoul. We need a more thorough system—a system that can voice all of the issues on the table together and make decisions based on the larger, long-term plans of the place and environment, not based on such short term popularity. For the Han River it is especially urgent because the river is an extremely important part of the city. Politicians are planning to do projects here and there without sufficient information that could give more clarity to the overall direction of the project. As an architect, I would like to suggest restoration as a reasonable direction for the development of the Han River and its edge area.

> RP: So what about the Han River? How do you see its relationship to the future of the city? Will it still be the kind of economic engine that it once was, instilled in the psyche of the city as such? Or is it now an orphan of a former era?

BC: I see it very positively. I think it is fortunate for Seoul that the river's edge is on a flood plain, and that it has not been developed much yet. Throughout the 1970s and 1980s, many parts of Seoul went through thoughtless urban interventions. But now, both the general public and the administrators of Seoul have become much more conscious. After fifty years of hard work, Korea is a stronger economic power and has greater enthusiasm toward constructing better places, especially with the completion of the Cheonggycheon project—the removal of an elevated expressway to reveal a waterway with walking path, a persuasive urban development that was accepted by the general public as a very successful project.

Besides the river project, there are two other major restoration projects in Seoul to deal with in the very near future. One is a large parcel of land that has been occupied by the U.S. military for the last few decades. The other is the 110-acre train depot. Both of these projects present large opportunities for the city and will happen in the next few years. The river project should be looked at in relation to all of these ensuing developments. The military site will be used as a public park and the train depot site as a business center. They are all within walking distance of the Han River. I see the Han River project as a great opportunity not only for Seoul but also Korea, Asia, and the world. I believe it could play a role as an engine for great future developments in Seoul, that is if the project gets developed thoughtfully and properly.

> RP: Indeed, the Cheonggycheon was a milestone, an example for cities everywhere of the development potential of restorative infrastructure projects—not just for questions of urban aesthetics and public education, but as crucial urban economic engines. Regarding any project related to the waterfront, now the looming new global consideration has to do with climate change and sea level rise, not to mention the potential for

energy generation and the like. Seoul could again be at the forefront of these issues with its Han River considerations. Do you feel that your Harvard studies can point to some directions within this realm? What are the next steps relative to developing a public awareness of the possibilities and public debate on the long-term viability of a large city on a large river?

BC: The Han is a large river, and Seoul is a large city. The next step relative to developing a public awareness would be to create a forum with various fields of expertise to offer different strategies. But educating the authorities, and, increasingly, the general public who vote them into office, would be fundamental. Establishing a public organization, with groups of experts and consultants, to provide the underlying paradigm, values, regulations, and review boards that could be widely accepted by the citizens.

As architects and urban designers, we could talk, write, publish, exhibit, and create events for the general public to view proposals that are on the table. Perhaps we could generate a road map for incremental growth and development or a vision of what Seoul might be in the next fifty or one hundred years. This is important for the city; the people of Seoul would have a voice in its future. Essentially, we, as architects and urban designers, need to establish various means of communicating with the people and the authorities.

Since the 1960s, we have been noticing the more active use of rivers for the improvement of cities or urban life. What are some cases of cities that made good use of their rivers, in your opinion? Can you think of some specific waterfront or water-related projects? What are some things that have been missed even in these projects or water-related projects in general? What kind of architectural research, study, or proposal can be done in a big-city context like Seoul and the Han River, and how? I would like to hear your comments from the view of an urban designer or architect.

RP: Certainly in Western Europe and North America there has been a proliferation of riverfront redevelopment strategies—in just about any major city that one can think of. This, of course, in some respects is a direct reflection of the real estate market, and the obsolescence of shipping and industrial uses along navigable waterways, opening up the possibilities for recreational and residential uses. Given our growing cultural proclivity for "waterfront" at all cost, high-end residential areas and parks have been the resultant by-product. In

New York, projects like Battery Park City, built on land-fill, have reflected this tendency.

It was not always this way. A century ago in New York City, it was Central Park that was the residential "waterfront"—or "greenfront" actually—and the most desired location for the cultural elite. This is still true, but the water edge real estate is heating up, especially for the striving upper-middle class. Decades ago, Riverside Park on the Hudson also represented a similar phenomenon, but today, waterfront redevelopment is far more pervasive, to the point that Donald Trump was able to replace the last functioning rail yard in Manhattan on the Upper West Side with housing. Yet it is not a foregone conclusion that rail will never again be strategic. Herein lies some of the danger of being rather shortsighted in rushing to discard irreplaceable infra-structure for the purpose of the easy profits presently coming from "luxury" waterfront.

For riverfront strategies, the San Antonio River-walk project, which dates from the 1970s, is considered an iconic precedent. Now the strategy has moved to Cleveland, for example, and Pittsburgh, and Toronto (actually "lakefront"). In Europe, Amsterdam has perhaps redeveloped its waterfront on the largest scale. But there is also Antwerp, which represents a very interesting experience (positive and negative) that even much larger cities like Seoul might learn from. Barcelona's waterfront transformation (actually "seafront") is perhaps most impressive of all, from the point of view of the creation of public space and urban recreation possibilities.

I think one of the crucial pieces left out of all of these projects has to do with the ecological equation, especially the rising sea levels that, at least for New York, have begun to intercept the discourse. And of course, in Bangkok the problem is already drastic, having to do with both a sinking city and rising water. There is no way that these issues can be explored without the hand of the designer, and without serious research to integrate science. And to date, not much has been done anywhere. But things can change pretty quickly. It's an interesting chemistry that engages spatial poetry and eco-science.

1 Since the late '90s the Seoul Metropolitan Government has variously promoted Seoul as an innovative global capital. The "Basic Urban Plan" for Seoul, originally enacted in 1966, has been revised several times, including the 2006 version that targeted development up to 2020, with a heightened emphasis on "sustainable development." In this period, completion of the Cheonggyecheon River redevelopment definitively thrust the city into international prominence as a planning innovation hub. And other preservation efforts encompass diverse fabrics such as the traditional Insa-dong commercial street and more recently, the monumental Seun-sangga megastructure from the '60s. The planning of the Han River redevelopment expand these precedents. The urban design studios were twice invited to explore large redevelopment sites; in Spring 2006 focusing on the Cheonggyecheon River corridor and on the the Dongdaemun Stadiums area, and in Spring 2015 focusing on large redevelopment sites in Suwon City within the larger Seoul region. The Earth Institute Urban Design Lab also completed a study for a new town at Dongtan in the Seoul region. See *Dongtan-2: A Premise for Urban Living*, ed. Richard Plunz, Richard Gonzalez, and Leo Daehwan Chung (New York: Columbia University Earth Institute Urban Design Lab, August 2009).

This interview was made with Seoul architect Byoung-soo Cho in Spring 2006 in Cambridge when he was teaching at the Harvard University Graduate School of Design.

Crossing Paths 1966–70

"Crossing Paths 1966–70," talk presented at *Urbanism Is Everybody's Business: A Celebration of the Shadrach Woods Archive* at Avery Library, Columbia University Graduate School of Architecture, Planning, and Preservation, November 14, 2005.

Troy, New York, Market Square

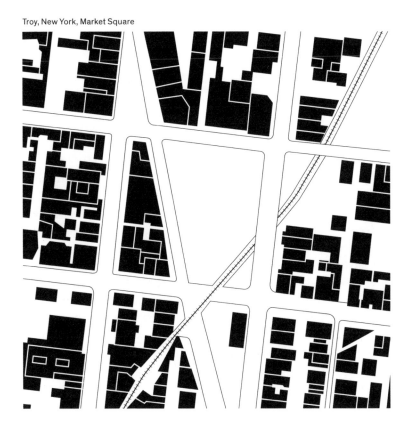

The risk in this exercise is superficiality—dredging up interpretations of things for which little evidence, or little possibility of corroboration, exists. It is not so easy to unearth material from a past context to another today. As students, we found it curious that Shadrach Woods was an American, but that his contribution was entirely framed by a practice in Paris, and we wondered why mainstream architectural culture in the States cared so little. I was a student at Rensselaer Polytechnic Institute in Troy, New York.[1] For that period there is little accessible public record to go on—although Kenneth Frampton and Alessandra Latour did explore the notion that Rensselaer was the American "Team 10 School" of the sixties in an essay in *Lotus* 27.[2] Having attended the university for the duration of three degrees—engineering, architecture, and urbanism—and having taught there briefly, I can affirm that their assessment was more or less correct, and it is an appropriate jumping-off point tonight.

Frampton and Latour discussed some of the circumstances that led to the dominance of Team 10 thinking at Rensselaer, especially in the advanced studios—having to do with a particular conjunction of students and young faculty. Also important to note was the presence of an acting dean with tremendous breadth and intelligence, who understood the great significance of the new tendencies in Europe relative to the situation in the United States.[3] Team 10 members and associates were frequently visiting critics. Rensselaer was fertile ground for planting the ideas of that amazing group, who by the mid-'60s had managed to create a new discourse within European architecture—indeed a new field within design related to "urbanisme" (with an "e")—and one far more inclusive than what by then had became known as "urban design" in the United States. Embedded in Team 10 ideals was the search for new languages that were capable of bridging design and the applied sciences in a way that reached beyond the "form follows function" rubric of the modern movement.

Among the central figures of Team 10, it was Woods who really connected with us. He was the most important theoretician of that group. What he built attracted us immensely, for he was not only able to get large things done, but managed to express the vital ideas of the projects—the scale of the social vision was not lost in the marketplace. There was simply nothing like his practice here in the U.S. We were very taken with, for example, the ATBAT work of the mid-'50s in Casablanca—the concerns of my final thesis project (made with Alberto Cardenas and William Dumka) could be traced directly to it. Our thesis project was for the extension of the town of Zaghouan in Tunisia, about an hour and a half from the capital.[4] We very consciously chose this topic as a sequel to ATBAT, and to Woods' more recent work in Chad for the extension of Fort Lamy (1962, now named N'Djamena). With the idea to follow in Woods' footsteps, we were put in touch with a Peace Corps worker in Zaghouan, and received the requisite documentation. Of course we did not exactly do footsteps—we deviated considerably.

But it was Woods' ATBAT and those remarkable reinterpretations of the local culture of housing—a kind of exercise in built anthropology—that had come to interest us. Woods' somewhat later invention of the "stem" principle—especially its application to the extension of Fort Lamy—was also of great interest. The question of formal language was very important. We were seduced not only by the anthropological genesis of that work, but also by its plasticity. It managed somehow to capture the informality of a local vernacular, resulting in a new kind of "modern." The ATBAT and Fort Lamy work was not well known in the States, but we devoured foreign publications—the *Dutch Forum* was indispensable—and Rensselaer had a particularly good working library for architecture. I should also mention George Wittenborn's remarkable bookstore on Madison Avenue where everything was available, including of course *Le Carré Bleu*.

For our design of the Zaghouan housing system, we also looked elsewhere. We were very interested in John F. C. Turner's ideas that deployed strategies of self-built infill toward an alternative kind of "vernacular," more liberated from aestheticization and responsive to the informal sector economic context. The August 1963 issue of *Architectural Design* was very important in that it expanded the boundaries of housing "design" to include the informal sector—with what was then an amazing documentation by Turner of the urbanization process in Lima, Peru. The notion of the "informal" was also embedded in Woods' "stem," which we saw as a kind of anti-master plan intended to permit flexibility in growth and change.

As useful to us as "stem" was the notion of "web," which Woods developed only slightly later. Its deployment in the Frankfurt central area redevelopment plan (1963) and then the Free University of Berlin campus extension (1963) opened up a new window for us. We ended up siting our Zaghouan fabric within a "micro-web" of streets, services, and other infrastructure, which would be coined a "sites and services" strategy by the World Bank in the '80s. With the appearance of the *Team 10 Primer* (1965), both "stem" and "web" were placed within the larger context of Team 10 consolidated from several previous issues of *Architectural Design*. Here in the States, the *Primer* was somewhat of an "underground" publication, and it totally absorbed us.

It legitimized our interests. Through it we were transformed from our own relatively provincial context to another world of substantial ideas and debate—and to the otherworldly context of the Dubrovnik café, so prominently featured on the cover.

At the time, we were also well aware of other related projects employing similar strategies, including Le Corbusier's Venice hospital (1964–66). I remember discussing whether or not Corbusier also owed something of Venice to Woods, and the Situationists too. We could well imagine that in the mid-sixties the Paris scene was rather tight. Chandigarh was not so useful—it was already a dated scheme (1950). It invoked a scale, which seemed to discredit the inherent interest of the approach, beyond its lyric compositional qualities. We were more interested in fabric than grand gesture.

In 1968, Woods published the office monograph, *Candilis Josic Woods: Building for People*. Its appearance represented a defining moment for us, satisfying a pent-up demand for documentation. His "complete works" were finally available in consolidated form. We had a pattern book, and discussed it as such—and how it would replace Le Corbusier's *Oeuvre Complête*, which up to that moment was the requisite resource for studio work (even if we were getting a little fed up with him). Perhaps the most interesting part of this story is what happens "next." While there remained another two or three years of vicarious Woods-related activity at Rensselaer, it disappeared with the exodus of particular faculty and the entrance of a new dean, who felt the school should return to "Architecture" with a capital "A"—architecture for art's sake.

We were studying in a very complex moment. For us, perhaps the two most important critical works on urbanism of the decade came from the American postwar deurbanist diaspora— Jane Jacobs' *The Death and Life of Great American Cities* (1961) and Serge Chermayeff and Christopher Alexander's *Community and Privacy: Toward an Architecture of Humanism* (1963). Jacobs' critique verified the extreme pathological deurbanist strategies that we saw being played out in the streets. But it was the architect Chermayeff's critique of the new "consumer urbanism" of the suburbs that was truly a breath of fresh air in the midst of dreadful corporate practice and its apologists at the "height of empire." Chermayeff and Alexander broke new ground with the first applied digital design model, incorporated into the book's methodology. In fact, *Community and Privacy* is still extremely relevant—perhaps now more than ever. Chermayeff, by the way, was a fervent admirer of Woods—a distinction shared by very few. As an aside, our other hero was Louis Kahn—so it was Chermayeff/ Woods/Kahn.[5]

I was interested in urbanism as it related to the development of cybernetic theory at the beginning of the Information Age—still a remarkable heritage—with the work of figures like Ross Ashby and Norbert Wiener. After my year or so of teaching, it was apparent that the Chermayeff and Alexander digital methodologies merged with Woods' ideas. It further developed the deployment of the intermediate design language pioneered by Chermayeff—to negotiate between the sociological, digital, and built formal outcomes. It was a kind of naïve "structuralism," which was also evolving within Woods thinking—what Jean-Louis Violeau has characterized as an "oscillation between *rules* and *behavior*"—"a trilogy of *place, moment, architecture.*"[6]

Michael Harrington's *The Other America* (1962), and Frantz Fanon's *The Wretched of the Earth* (1965 in English) introduced the immediacy of post-colonial poverty in Africa and a certain equivalent underclass amid the popular perception of great wealth in the States. They are still extremely relevant books— again, perhaps now more than ever. They contributed greatly to our interest in activism, and on this account, we began to move beyond the discretionary concerns of Team 10. The sands were shifting. Even the powerful American corporate practice at the "height of empire" was in question. We couldn't believe that the Museum of Modern Art would actually entertain Bernard Rudofsky's remarkable "Architecture Without Architects" exhibition (1965). We ran down to get the catalog as inspiration for the Zaghouan project. I remember how enraged some of the establishment was at the proposition of "without architects," which they deemed to be anti-professional. Within this power flux, we began to develop our own student identity. We had the *Gorgon* as an "alternative" publication—with a more positivist outlook than *Novum Organum* at Yale. Student exchange grew between both schools.

When the so-called events of May '68 finally arrived, *Le Carré Bleu* was ready—but so were we. Like others, I continued to teach. Teaching was the only way to avoid combat in Vietnam. But the force of events moved teaching out of the university and into the city. At Penn State, I began our work in Mantua in Philadelphia—one of the most violent enclaves on the East Coast at that moment. In spite of the political cacophony, we were still very interested in architectural design, and we wanted to change what architecture was and how it was done. We reclaimed an abandoned house to live and work in, and began our work with the Mantua Community Planners. We worked alongside teachers and children to build the Mantua Middle School in an abandoned factory—the existing local public school was hopelessly mediocre and over capacity. This was our new kind of "architecture." *Connection* from Harvard University's Graduate School of Design published the work with the title "Building with People"—a reference to Woods' *Building for People.*[7] Woods was still a referent, but he was absorbed in conventional academia at Harvard—we were not.

Over a two-year period we also completed the project for the digital modeling of environmental change in Mantua, built on the groundwork laid by Chermayeff and Alexander—an impassioned response to the pathology found all around us and to the desperate need for change. But still there was continuity in our experience. When the work was to be published by the U.S. Public Health Service we chose *Mantua Primer*, a reference to the *Team 10 Primer.*[8] Team 10 was still with us. We endlessly scrutinized Giancarlo De Carlo's beautiful study for Urbino (1966 in Italian).[9] We saw in new terms the value of history. In our minds Urbino and Mantua (even if in Philadelphia) were equally deserving.

So Woods—in fact all of Team 10—did continue to "wander like a ghost" through our work; they still do. It's true, even, that if "twenty years is not enough," the same can be said for forty. I can imagine that is why we are here tonight.

1 Troy, New York and Rensselaer have long occupied a place of special importance for me, given my family history in the city, dating back to 1808 with pioneering industrial and scientific enterprises. By the 1960s Troy, once a vital and urbane place, was in a pathological state of decline.

2 Kenneth Frampton and Alessandra Latour, "Notes on American Architectural Education: From the End of the Nineteenth Century Until the 1970s," *Lotus International* 27 (1980): 5–39.

3 It's important to mention that acting dean Donald Mochon, Robert Winne, Michael Mostoller, and Andrej Pinno all worked in Woods' office in Paris.

4 Richard Plunz, "Zagouhan, Tunisia: Proposal for a Town in Tunisia," *Gorgon* 12 (January 1967).

5 See my review of Alessandra Latour's *Louis I. Kahn: L'Uomo, Il Maestro* (1986) in *Design Book Review* 21 (Summer 1991): 9–10.

6 Jean-Louis Violeau, "Rules versus Behavior: in Search of an Inhabitable World," in Tom Avermaete et al., *Team 10: Between Modernity and the Everyday* (Delft, NL: Delft University of Technology, 2003), 171–78.

7 Richard Plunz, "Mini-School: Building With People," *Connection* VI, no.3 (Spring 1969).

8 Richard Plunz, *Mantua Primer: Toward a Program for Environmental Change* (Baltimore, MD: United States Public Health Service, 1970); Also see Richard Plunz, "Reflections on 'From Penn State to San Leucio and Back'," in *Eugenio Battisti. Storia, Critica, Progetto Nella Continuita Della Ricerca*, ed. Antonio Piva Pierfranco Galliani (Rome: Gangemi, 2009), 51–52.

9 Giancarlo Carlo de Carlo, *Urbino: The History of a City and Plans for its Development*, trans. Loretta Schaeffer Guarda (Cambridge, MA: MIT Press, 1970).

Scratching the Surface

Excerpted from "Remediation as Urban Development Strategy: Scratching the Surface," in *Eco-Gowanus: Urban Remediation by Design*, ed. Patricia Culligan and Richard Plunz. (New York: Columbia University Graduate School of Architecture, Planning, and Preservation, 2007), 24–31.

Brooklyn, Gowanus, Public Place

Brooklyn's Gowanus Canal had long been considered one of the most toxic urban water bodies in North America.[1] It was the adjacent community that requested our earliest study, beginning in the fall of 2003, which probed the entire Gowanus basin.[2] Our second study, beginning in the fall of 2004, focused on the Public Place site. The first study set the stage for strategic thinking relative to canal restoration as a total urban development process. The second study was more specific in terms of remediation needs and techniques that focused on a single parcel, augmented by the availability of additional geo-environmental engineering input.

The sensibilities of both studies broke new ground. Our concerns prioritized remediation as more than simply "cleansing"—i.e., the preparation of a parcel of land for rebuilding preliminary to normative development practice. Instead we envisioned remediation as a continuum and an integral part of future urban site programming and development. An important consideration in justifying this approach is the high cost of remediation itself, which, as an investment, logically requires maximizing positive secondary impacts. We proposed that the remediation process develop techniques to minimize attrition relative to that investment. Typically, present remediation sites in urban environments are minimally cleansed in the anticipation of relatively low-level uses, with the attendant problem that the low-level uses are fixed for an unforeseeable future. To date, the model for the Gowanus has consisted of the minimal removal of contaminated soil followed by site "capping" in the form of parking surfaces adjacent to generic "big box" retail, tending to lock in similar low-level uses on adjacent land parcels and sealing the fate of the entire canal.

We struck a responsive chord with our community partners relative to these concerns, especially given growing community opposition to the present range of proposals for the canal—the "big box" phenomenon, as well as the somewhat fanciful proposals for upscale Gowanus "waterfront" condominium projects. In regard to the latter, at the beginning of our work, residents seemed evenly split between "housing" and the continuity of industrial use along the canal. Industrial continuity gained more credibility with community stakeholders as our work progressed. Their primary concerns pointed to the Gowanus as an irreplaceable piece of New York City infrastructure, and that far too much of this infrastructure had been lost during the past five decades, along with the countless middle-income livelihoods that the infrastructure supported. This loss of jobs has greatly contributed to income stratification in the city. Our Gowanus proposals argued against a blind acceptance of these simplistic forms of infrastructural displacement, which substitute the diversity of old infrastructure with a "mono-functional" residential economy.

The older global cities that remain competitive will be the ones that plan wisely for the new global order. This consideration must engage climate change, especially for ocean-based metropolitan areas like New York. Studies for the New York metropolitan region predict that by the year 2100, storm surges will reach 14 feet (4.3m) and will recur on four-year intervals.[3] Such scenarios arrive squarely at the pragmatics of redevelopment for the Gowanus. Flooding along the canal has always been a problem— the removal of the natural marsh of the Gowanus Creek has limited the distribution of surges. The tropical storm that occurred on October 13, 2005, was typical, with the area around Second and Sackett Streets under both water and sewage from the combined sewer overflow (CSO) problem.[4] Such flooding is expected on increasingly frequent intervals. As the environmental standards governing the release of raw sewage increase, the primitive one-pipe systems will become less and less acceptable. Given that building an entirely new two-pipe infrastructure is not economically feasible, a micro-scale approach to storm-water interception will be the only recourse.

In post-industrial New York City, the real estate industry has dominated the growth of the economy for both the residential and service sectors, as a component of the F.I.R.E. (Finance, Insurance, and Real Estate) based economy. This dominance has evolved for well over a half-century.[5] Old industrial sites adjacent to water are of particular interest, since their disuse does not present undue social and environmental complications relative to existing community issues. And "water" is highly marketable. From this point of view, the Gowanus can be considered attractive. First of all, it is "waterfront," in spite of the canal's severe degradation. Indeed, because of the degradation, Gowanus promises to be "cheap waterfront"—especially if remediation is somehow minimized or if the remediation costs are borne by the public sector. The attractiveness of "cheap waterfront" is enhanced considerably by its location relative to the relentless gentrification of the surrounding upscale neighborhoods, Park Slope and Carroll Gardens. The amenities and transportation options of Fifth Avenue in Park Slope and Smith Street in Carroll Gardens are only ten or fifteen minutes away from the canal by foot. In the world of hype, created by realtors, the fantasy of "Venice on the Canal" lies close at hand.[6] For the Gowanus remediation, however, we found that an emphasis on developing both high-level uses and long-term outlooks would necessitate prioritizing "production" over "dormitory" uses.

Our considerations also prioritized the growing social inequity between those participating in the post-industrial affluence and those increasingly marginalized. In this regard, the Gowanus can be seen as a microcosm of New York and its future societal challenges. In the past four decades, most solid working-class jobs have disappeared, and the canal basin has been left with increasingly high- and low-income disparity with the loss of its demographic "middle." The most blatant symbol of this condition is pervasive gentrification, with increasingly affluent ownership of the existing housing stock, construction of new upper middle income condos, and higher rentals. An obvious side effect is a lack of affordable housing production for those who should benefit most. Nothing "trickles down" to the bottom. Not coincidentally, those left out are the same people who suffer as their "old economy" jobs disappear.

We have envisioned a certain continuity of use, moving from the present period of industrial abandonment to a next period of remediation integrated with research and development, and then to a third period of sustained new industry driven by spin-offs from remediation technology. This strategy prioritizes gaining a new "industrial" base for New York after many decades of neglect—one that is capable of hybridizing product reuse of remaining industrial sites spawning a long-term urban restoration industry. This future would be intertwined with urban micro-infrastructure related to waste disposal, energy production, and natural resources (especially water)—all largely self-sustaining in the urban context, evoking entirely new concepts of what urban "production" actually means, pointing toward new forms of urban "industry" that integrate with the remediation process itself. This trajectory engages what has been popularly described as a new field of "restoration ecology" and is corollary with degraded urban contexts—and therefore has the potential to generate a new urban "restoration economy."[7] The restoration economy is becoming a key component in the reinvention of urban economies as restoration science moves toward an urban "natural" environment, following the logic that degraded urban ecosystems provide more economic opportunities than detriments.[8] Involved are emerging forms of "nature" as a resource and an "accumulation strategy," including the "spent nature" of brownfields. Nature is redefined such that degraded and consumed environments are seen as a powerful new frontier of capital accumulation: "nature is increasingly if selectively replicated as its own marketplace."[9] The social and monetary costs and benefits must factor into this expanded arena of considerations, moving away from normative real estate development models.

Embedded in the concept of this new urban production is a critique of the premises of "economic growth" that have been inherited from the industrial era. The old models rely on strategies that assume infinitely expanding material consumption fueled by always growing economies. Also characteristic is a separation of economics from ecology, with economists ignoring natural contexts, and ecologists ignoring human contexts—a formulation that no longer guarantees human betterment. By contrast, urban economies that thrive in the new era will have to function within a "post-economic" realm that rejects the "canonical assumptions" of insatiable wants and infinite resources leading to supposed "growth forever."[10] The Gowanus represents a prime example of what this means. Remediation to the highest possible use will necessitate the conservation of resources, including the infrastructure itself. Remediation will entail more than a mute stage set for the expediency of "growth" on the cheap—that is, simple low-level re-urbanization without the maximum return in both social and economic terms. In this new formulation, the remediation of the Gowanus to maximum possibilities of use can pay off far beyond the necessary additional costs, and indeed, the ecological remediation itself becomes the basis for the new era of redefined production.

For the Gowanus basin, the remediation techniques required to arrive at new "maximum" use options will exceed state-of-the-art remediation practice and associated monetary requirements. The scale and fragmentation of contamination is such that the investment will have to entail a new long-term public-private conception coordinated over a large number of site parcels. Given eighty years of intense industrial activity spread along the two-mile corridor and the period of petrochemical uses, what exists today is an archaeological patchwork of unknown scale and hazards. As in classical archaeology, study of the Gowanus contamination must combine empirical forensics with received historical knowledge. In this there are lessons to be learned from recent developments in the archaeological sciences.[11] For our purposes, our study characterized the residual pollutants from this historical layering in three primary categories: BTEX, PAHs, and heavy metals, but whose underground behaviors could only be approximated within severe limits given the extraordinary number of unknowns below the ground surface. These include underground water flows, precise geologic formations, and the intensity of the original pollutant sources (in this case, releases dating back to more than a century ago). For the Gowanus basin, the pattern of contamination elicits as many unknowns as does the economics of its remediation. Indeed, we have just "scratched the surface," literally and figuratively.

Science aside, the primary language for our studies has entailed "design," deployed as a catalytic urban tool—the only effective means of visualizing for public discourse the complexities of the urban intervention strategies that our research has evoked.[12] For some readers the complexity of our vision will simply affirm that primitive "cap and pave" strategies will be the manifest destiny of the canal—the path of least resistance, given the many unknowns at hand. But others will recognize the value of research that explores alternative visions—more difficult in the short term, but more beneficial in the long term. It is the latter group to whom our studies speak.

1 The struggle to clean up the Gowanus basin culminated with its designation as a national Superfund site in 2010, with an estimated cost of over $500 million, after a contentious period of negotiation between city, private market, and national interests—all still very much at play in 2016.

2 In Fall 2003 and Fall 2004, Columbia Urban Ecology Studios were commissioned to work on remediation and redevelopment of the Gowanus Canal in Brooklyn, the largest brownfield site in New York City, eventually designated as a Superfund site by the federal government. A third Urban Ecology Studio also examined the site in Fall 2010.

3 Cynthia Rosenzweig and William D. Solecki, "Climate Change and a Global City: The Potential Consequences of Climate Variability and Change, Metro East Coast" (New York: Columbia Earth Institute, 2001). The author also consulted Vivien Gornitz, Klaus Jacob, and Cynthia Rosenzweig, "Vulnerability of the New York City Metropolitan Area to Coastal Hazards, Including Sea Level Rise: Inferences for Urban Coastal Risk Management and Adaptation Policies," unpublished manuscript.

4 Documented by Friends of the Greater Gowanus (FROGG), email to author and constituents, October 14, 2005; a similar event also documented by FROGG via email, July 10, 2006.

5 For an early assessment of the impact of the F.I.R.E. phenomenon, see Robert Fitch, The Assassination of New York (London and New York: Verso, 1993).

6 Recent press coverage on the inflation of Gowanus real estate includes: Jeff Vandam, "Some See Venice; Some See a Canal," New York Times, October 30, 2005, 11; Joseph Berger, "From Open Sewer to Open for Gentrification; Many Gowanus Residents Want Its Color to Remain Blue," New York Times, November 28, 2005, B-1; Lisa Chamberlain, "A Suburban Builder Heads to the City," New York Times, April 5, 2006, C7.

7 The restoration economy concept is well summarized in Storm Cunningham, The Restoration Economy: The Greatest New Growth Frontier (San Francisco: Berrett-Koehler Publishers, Inc., 2002).

8 The economics of the new eco-enterprise is well analyzed in Herman E. Daley and Joshua Farley, Ecological Economics: Principles and Application (Washington, D.C.: Island Press, 2004).

9 On the historical shift in environmental capitalism, see Leo Panitch and Colin Leys, "Coming to Terms with Nature," Socialist Register 43 (London: The Merlin Press, 2006). In particular, see Neil Smith, "Nature Accumulation Strategy," Socialist Register 43, 16–36.

10 On "canonical assumptions," see Daley and Farley, Ecological Economics, xxi–xxii.

11 For important recent explorations on the correlation between archaeological and climatological science, see Eberhard Zangger, The Future of the Past: Archeology in the 21st Century (London: Phoenix, 2002).

12 Serge Chermayeff first defined the concept of "design as catalyst" in reference to urban and environmental design. See Serge Chermayeff, Design and the Public Good: Selected Writings, 1930–1980, ed. Richard Plunz (Cambridge MA: MIT Press, 1982), 289–95.

The Design Equation

Excerpted from *Urban Climate Change Crossroads*, ed. Richard Plunz and Maria Paola Sutto (New York: Columbia University Urban Design Lab, 2008). Republished by Ashgate Publishing Limited, Surrey, UK, 2010.

Rome, Piazza di Pietra

In reflecting on the Club of Rome and their initial 1972 publication, *The Limits to Growth: A Report for the Club of Rome's Project on the Predicament of Mankind*, one is still confronted by a very relevant document in terms of understanding the complexity of our present condition.[1] *Limits to Growth*, and later related studies, summarized for a whole generation a deep concern about the implications inherent to the society of consumption that was in evolution by the '60s. Indeed, especially in the United States, consumption was promoted as a new economic order in the postwar global reconfiguration. We tend to forget that the same debates today are far from new—only the immediacy is growing. For example, the Club of Rome predictions about CO_2 concentration were on the mark.

Consider the work of the British economist Ezra Mishan, also associated with the Club of Rome. Mishan provides a relevant critical perspective on the culture of consumption. His "Mishan Model," published in *The Costs of Economic Growth* in 1967, effectively demonstrates the limits of automobile culture.[2] Mishan's crucial judgment was that, even after public consensus would conclude that fewer automobiles would be socially preferable to transport dysfunction, the system will have no built-in controls— such that fewer automobiles would not be obtained without extraordinary intervention external to the transport sector. Using the automobile as a metaphor for our global growth in general, we can begin to understand the enormity of the questions surrounding global environmental change today—and that the growth of global consumption and environmental degradation is not easily reversed without unprecedented global intervention.

Mishan provided a paradigm for the "manifest destiny" of the so-called American Century, as global power has played itself out. Until very recently, in so many quarters, the American hegemony was expected to govern the planetary trajectory. In the run-up to the U.S. invasion of Iraq in 2004, President George W. Bush used the argument that there must be "…no holding back, no compromise, no hesitation" in protecting the American "way of life."[3] But evidence is well in place that the American way of life is itself not sustainable, made clear by the futility of the war itself and its connection to the growing depletion of the world's oil reserves that remain the crucial life support for the culture of consumption in the United States. Now the "American way of life" enters an excruciatingly difficult period, ultimately for the better. We know that within recorded history there is no precedent on a global scale for the environmental disruptions that now unfold. But in terms of relative scale—of human response—that's another very interesting question altogether. We are not alone in history. And in history there have been powerful precedents.

Among my favorite places in the world are the sites of the classical Greek cities of the southwest Aegean shore. Priene, in particular, is a place where one is invited to contemplate our present environmental dilemmas—and our human frailties, upheavals, and struggles. When one looks out from its promontory, across so many kilometers of green agricultural fields, one can't help but reflect on the souls that lived there millennia ago, and at what point those city-states felt the enormity of their ecological miscalculations.[4] They were too late in realizing that the deforestation that provided the material for their growth would also be the source of their destruction.

The Meander River silted over the harbors and the livelihoods of the cities that it had formerly nourished. Strabo documents how the citizens of Priene had already lost their port by his time (63 BC– AD 24). In fact, we know that Priene was moved to its present location in the fourth century BC, with the ruins of the earlier city still remaining today at some unknown location under the silt. I mention this because I think that understanding the adaptation question engages a huge historical dimension—one can even say that environmental adaptation has been a "normal" condition of human history—but one that is anathema to modern design culture.[5] We simply do not look back. Relative to this history, and especially to ecology, is it possible that we are now in a "post-historical period," when the easiness of the past is no longer so resonant? The brilliance of Bill McKibben's book *The End of Nature* was in the articulation of this point more than a decade ago.[6]

The gamble for ecological survival has always been reliant on technology and design—and when the technological limits are obvious, the design adaptation has to be made. As with the cities of the Meander, when design adaptation is inadequate, humankind has moved on. The design imperative appeared with Hurricane Katrina in New Orleans. Now New York faces a moment of truth with hurricanes and sea level rise. We have definitively arrived at the issue of "limits"—questions anticipated by the Club of Rome and now far more immediate.

Urban adaptation goes beyond building seawalls, moving from flood plains, inventing more robust infrastructures, and the like. A part of our consideration in terms of urbanism is the changing nature of urban enterprise. Urban climate change adaptation involves urban economies—and not just global, but also local economies—and new urban industry that can integrate with the process of adaptation itself. This trajectory engages what has been popularly described as a new field of "restoration ecology" and is corollary with degraded urban contexts. It therefore has the potential to generate a new urban production.

In cities, the restoration economy is increasingly critical—as restoration science moves from built fabric to the urban "natural environment," following the logic that degraded urban ecosystems may actually provide more economic opportunities than detriments.[7] Involved are emerging new forms of "natural" resources, including the "spent nature" of the brown fields. The concept of nature as "accumulation strategy" is expanding to include the redefinition of nature itself. Degraded and consumed environments are no longer seen as a liability, but rather as a powerful new frontier of capital accumulation—such that "nature is increasingly, if selectively, replicated as its own marketplace."[8] The social and monetary costs and benefits must factor this expanded arena of considerations, and this economic adaptation must go hand in hand with physical adaptation within climate strategies.

Embedded in the concept of new urban production is a critique of our inherited premises of "economic growth." The old models rely on the assumptions of always expanding material consumption fueled by always growing economies. Also characteristic is a separation of economics from ecology. Urban economies that thrive in the new era will have to function within a second modernity, the antithesis of the first that rejects the "canonical assumptions" of insatiable wants and infinite resources leading to supposed "growth forever."[9] Here we engage the question of a new beginning, and of climate change as a positive economic force. A positive prognosis is possible, especially if, as the German sociologist Ulrich Beck argues, now is a moment of a "second modernity," one "being born within the interstices of the first modernity, most of all within its cities..."[10]

When science interacts with the city, design is an essential catalyst. Geo-environmental analysis aside, the primary language for urban intervention has entailed "design" as a catalytic urban tool and an effective means of visualizing for public discourse the complexities of intervention strategies. The huge question is whether or not the design fields are adequately equipped to manage adaptation problems. Certainly the context for design activity is changing rapidly, but Western design culture has evolved over the past four or five centuries such that a change in trajectory on the scale of the ecological change that we now face will be challenging, to say the least.

Design is intimately connected to ecology, political science, and ultimately to the question of power—and the abuse of power. Yet design culture has always resisted forthright admission of this reality. For the "design equation" within the climate change challenge, I see this denial as complicit with the incapacity of the design world to deal with the environmental challenges intensified by climate change.

In the past one hundred fifty years or so, our present professional limitations have crystallized with the separation of architecture from engineering, the evolution of isolated design discourse and pedagogy, the artificial distinctions between design of buildings, urbanism, landscape, interiors, products, and the like. Today, there is a growing challenge to these institutionalized categories, not only from the changing nature of the problems, but also from new shared technologies of representation and production.

For decades, architecture had considered itself the "mother" activity for design of the built environment—even as it became more and more marginalized. During the present wave of global urbanization, this trend has intensified. The field has always accounted for a small percentage of the built environment, but in the new scale of global urbanization, it is minuscule. High architectural discourse has become more and more restricted to the world of high fashion. The problem is that high fashion is emblematic of the "mainstream" values of design culture—and a new legitimacy for design cannot be achieved simply through manifesto. There is a need for new fundamental design knowledge.

While the demand for built environment expertise is growing, the worldwide building industry is said to be the most extraordinarily wasteful and destructive of all human enterprise, placing it at the epicenter of any adaptation strategy. Of course the design marketplace itself is adapting to the new global context, including academia. But as the natural sciences "urbanize"—and they certainly are in our present wave of "glocalization"—urban science gets complicated, principally through the necessity for political engagement.

It is fortunate that new realities are coercing science and design into new relationships. The kind of creative process inherent to design methodologies, for so long anathema to the scientific "method," is suddenly gaining some notice and credibility from the science side. The problem, however, is reciprocity—and whether the superficial hermeticism that has come to characterize design discourse is able to meet this challenge. While the aesthete side of design culture is attempting to hold its own as an offshoot of the fashion industry, the cracks in this position are widening. This is especially true at the urban scale. There is a new evolving academic amalgam involving business, science, and design, deliberately blurred in response to new problem sets and scientific boundaries.

The momentum for this approach, at least in the United States, is quickly strengthening around the global warming phenomenon. But our centers of learning will have to wake up to realities beyond the attractions of new business models. And in spite of new visualization and fabrication tools, designers will have to acknowledge the reality that design culture seems to have regressed from its position in the '60s in terms of exploring a sustainable new "world model." Design culture needs to trace the same ground the natural sciences have already covered during the last four decades—and more.

1 Donella H. Meadows et al., *The Limits to Growth: A Report for the Club of Rome's Project on the Predicament of Mankind* (New York: Universe Books, 1972). This text was adapted from a talk given at the conference "Urban Climate Change Crossroads" held in Rome on February 4–5, 2008. The location lies within the formidable walls of the ancient Temple of Hadrian (145AD) adjacent to the Piazza di Pietra. The question of the "end of history" could be lost on no one.

2 E. J. Mishan, *The Costs of Economic Growth* (New York: Praeger Publishers, 1967).

3 President George W. Bush and British Prime Minister Tony Blair, remarks at The Cross Hall, November 20, 2003. (Washington, DC: The White House Office of the Press Secretary, 2005).

4 J. C. Kraft, et al., "Paleogeographic Reconstruction of Coastal Aegean Archeology Sites," *Science*, 195, 1977.

5 Within the field of archaeology, there is very interesting new work that correlates built form and climatological science. For example, see Eberhard Zangger, *The Future of the Past: Archaeology in the 21st Century* (London: Phoenix, 2002).

6 Bill McKibben, *The End of Nature* (New York: Random House, 1989).

7 For a summary of the restoration economy, see Storm Cunningham, *The Restoration Economy: The Greatest New Growth Frontier* (San Francisco: Berrett-Koehler Publishers, Inc., 2002); for an analysis of the economics of the new eco-enterprise, see Herman E. Daley and Joshua Farley, *Ecological Economics: Principles and Application* (Washington, D.C.: Island Press, 2004).

8 On the historical shift in environmental capitalism, see Leo Panitch and Colin Leys, "Coming to Terms with Nature," *Socialist Register* 43 (London: The Merlin Press, 2006). In particular, see Neil Smith, "Nature Accumulation Strategy," *Socialist Register* 43, 16–36.

9 On "canonical assumptions," see Daley and Farley, *Ecological Economics*, xxi–xxii.

10 Ulrich Beck and Johannes Willms, *Conversations with Ulrich Beck* (Cambridge, UK: Polity Press, 2004), 39, 183.

Garden City Redux?

Excerpted from "Garden City Redux?" in *Re-Cultivating the Garden City of Kumasi* (New York: Columbia University Urban Design Lab, 2012), 22–29.

Kumasi, Asawasi District

By 1970, Ghana's Volta River Dam Project was completed and acclaimed as retaining the world's largest artificial lake. But perhaps more significantly, the project accrued a vast array of urbanization anticipations and consequences.[1] It can be argued that today the discovery of offshore petroleum deposits will have a similar impact as Ghana embarks on its next phase of development. Oil exports are already feeding substantial GDP growth. For this reason, it is particularly important that the urbanization of the previous "water era" be well understood as we move forward into the "petroleum era."

During the "water era," Kumasi witnessed a large transformation from a regional capital of some 45,000 people in 1944 to a globalizing metropolis of over 1.6 million in 2010.[2] Viviana d'Auria's prodigious research documents the enormous impact of the Volta River project, including the trajectory of urbanization in Ghana and the role of the prevailing planning conventions of that period.[3] The question of Kumasi and its identification with the modernist concept of the English Garden City is brought to bear.[4] Within the constellation of issues we have faced in our work, an important one has been this elusive question of Garden City ideals within Kumasi's development, prominent toward the end of the Ghanaian colonial era and based on earlier antecedents in England.[5] Although this succession has been complicated to unravel, our considerations could not ignore this history—especially as the Garden City ideal may be reemerging in the Kumasi context, but in a significantly different form.

From its earliest settlement in the seventeenth century, Kumasi was notable for its location in the "garden" of the lush Ashante forest.[6] It was not until 1945 that the term "garden city" came into widespread use in Kumasi with the master plan for the city drawn up by Maxwell Fry and Jane Drew, subtitled "Garden City of West Africa." This appellation even remained in use in the period of independence after 1957. The correlation between Kumasi urbanism and the garden still remains today, for example in Kwasi Kwafo Adarkwa and John Post's study *The Fate of the Tree*.[7] The literal "garden" has long since been vastly reduced, given the tendency toward "urban landscape depletion" as documented by Victor Kwesi Quagraine and others.[8] So the question of the garden city arises yet again. Our work has attempted to explore the possible meanings of the "fate of the tree" in Kumasi culture, especially in the next phase of growth and development. Lurking deep within the culture of the city, before and now, there is something that resonates with its forest origins.

Our work has addressed what the "Garden City of Tomorrow" might be and how far we can stray from the colonial ideal before the original concept is meaningless. Our emphasis was on the restoration of the "natural" infrastructure of water and vegetation—still the lifeblood of the city—or whatever is left of it. But the larger unresolved question had to do with garnering the resources for restoration, not an easy question even for the wealthiest of cities. It became obvious that our restoration considerations had to entail something more than money. It had to involve the power of human capital and the energy of the so-called informal sector, destined to continue to dominate Kumasi's urbanization. It is estimated that 75 percent of the local workforce is employed in the informal sector.[9]

There has been substantial learning since 1945, when, for example, Fry and Drew planned a new residential district at Asawasi, not far from our Akorem-Adukrom-Sawaba site. Their scheme, dominated by formalized geometries of barracks-type housing, was imposed on the older, informal circulation pattern.[10] In the sixty years that ensued, a dense new layer of informal urbanization in contrast to the formal geometries emerged. Perhaps all that survives of Fry and Drew is their innovation in construction materials—the hand-produced cement-block production now prevalent everywhere in the city. By contrast, there was never formal planning at Akorem-Adukrom-Sawaba.

It was within the question of informality that we began our explorations, and the Asawasi precedent indicated just how much we had to learn. Even the term "informal" indicates our ignorance of a system that does not function within the financial and cultural constructs of our "formal" tenure. That the "informal" is another "formal" may be obvious, but given the limited range of our development tools, we don't even know how to understand exactly what it is. The "informal" is an extremely effective system that must be understood and respected. Significant to this understanding is the diverse land tenure system in Kumasi, with a large amount of "Stool Lands" remaining from before colonial law. Akorem-Adukrom-Sawaba lies within this tenure system.[11]

We studied seven urban "provocations," which grapple with a myriad of issues: the stewardship of water and processing of waste, the restoration of vegetation as part and parcel of a production economy, the harnessing of the energy of market economies, the retention of invaluable older investments like the railroad, and the envisioning of a new social net. The strategies are also varied: recycling human waste, containing sprawl, revitalizing railway infrastructure, strengthening community, activating cultural capital, harnessing the marketplaces, and empowering women. All prioritize innovation toward economic development.

In a sense, our focus might be seen as a logical extension of certain concerns of the founding faculty at the Kwame Nkrumah University of Science and Technology (KNUST), where we have enjoyed a collaboration to define the scope of our work. These concerns were summarized in 1966, in an issue of *Arena*, then the influential journal of the Architectural Association in London. It was entirely devoted to teaching and research within the KNUST faculty of architecture, founded only eight years earlier. The *Arena* number appeared on the cusp of the post-colonial era and looked to emerging new realities. The contributors were all variously involved with urban design in Kumasi, and they managed to capture the energy of this transitional moment. Represented was a trajectory found in some of the student projects for "Kumasi 2000," described as having all of the trappings of the then "developed" world:

> ... a wide-ranging familiarity with urban, industrial concepts; multi-level parking, overpasses, pedestrian zones, large scale air conditioning. Markets, of course, figure most prominently in the plan; at its apex stand a theatre, a hotel with a swimming pool, two cinemas, office towers, an open air restaurant, department stores, shopping arcades, a supermarket ...[12]

But there was also hesitation. The above fantasies stood in contrast to other curriculum concerns that had more to do with how to move from "today" to "towards tomorrow," with mention of an exhibition of the same theme, involving more work within an anthropological frame. In our own work, we came to understand that their "tomorrow" of today, some forty-seven years later, is much changed, and the question of our "tomorrow" remains difficult. We can only reflect on how our work will be viewed in another half century. Hopefully this work responds to the words of caution in the final essay of *Arena* by the prominent Ghanaian architect John Owusu-Addo and the African American architect J. Max Bond, then a young visiting faculty member at KNUST and for many years thereafter a prominent member of the Columbia faculty:

> We must have some idea of what progress should mean. Should we strive for individual luxury which a few will get anyway or should we concentrate on public facilities? What balance should be struck between the private and public spheres of one's environment? ... How will we design buildings which we can afford with our present very limited means but will not become obsolete as standards and means increase, and habits change? ... How can we do anything and yet allow for change?[13]

These are still vital questions in the Kumasi context. We have not arrived at "answers" in the same way that the Garden City once did. We have only managed to translate our learning into "provocations" that may speak more to the next generation of power and influence than the previous. As far as Garden City is concerned, it may not be too late for Kumasi, but the hour seems close at hand.

1 Viviana d'Auria and Bruno De Meulder, "Dam[ned] Landscapes: Re-envisioning the Volta River Project's Unsettled Territories," *Journal of Landscape Architecture* (Autumn 2011): 54–69.
2 Clifford Amoako and David Korboe, "Historical Development, Population Growth and Present Structure of Kumasi," in *Future of the Tree: Towards Growth and Development of Kumasi*, ed. Kwasi Kwafo Adarkwa (Kumasi, GH: University Printing Press, Kwame Nkrumah University of Science and Technology, 2011), 40–41.
3 Viviana d'Auria, "Developing Urbanism[s] in Development: Five Episodes in the Making of the Volta River Project in [Post]-Colonial Ghana 1945–76" (unpublished doctoral dissertation, Katholieke Universiteit Leuven, 2012).
4 Ebenezer Howard, *Garden Cities of To-morrow* (London: S. Sonnenschein & Co, 1902).
5 The Spring 2012 Urban Design Studio was commissioned to work in Kumasi, with a field study group visiting in January and confronting the remnants of a British colonial plan dominated by post-colonial informal development.
6 Thomas J. Lewin, *Asante before the British: The Prempean Years, 1875–1900* (Lawrence, KS: The Regents Press of Kansas, 1978), 9–11.
7 Kwasi Kwafo Adarkwa and Johan Post, *The Fate of the Tree: Planning and Managing the Development of Kumasi, Ghana* (Accra: Woeli Publishing Services, 2001).
8 Victor Kwesi Quagraine, "Urban Landscape Depletion in the Kumasi Metropolis," in *The Fate of the Tree*, 212–13.
9 Sam Afrane and George Ahiable, "The Informal Economy and Microfinance in Kumasi," in *The Fate of the Tree*, 112–113.
10 A. Graham Tipple, *The Development of Housing Policy in Kumasi, Ghana, 1901 to 1981, with an Analysis of the Current Housing Stock* (Newcastle: Centre for Architectural Research and Development Overseas, University of Newcastle upon Tyne, 1987), 12–14.
11 D.N.A. Hammond, "Land Tenure and Land Policy," in *The Fate of the Tree*, 82.
12 Ayi Kwei, "The Human Material," *Arena: Architectural Association Journal* 82, (July–August, 1966): 45.
13 John Owusu-Addo and Max Bond, "Aspirations," *Arena*, 62.

Vagaries of Deterritorialization

Excerpted from "Vagaries of Deterritorialization" in *Reimagining Lutyens' Delhi* (New York: Columbia University Urban Design Lab, 2014), 2–4.

New Delhi, Connaught Place

Ironically, in spite of its simplistic spatial configuration, the future of Edwin Lutyens' Delhi seems complicated—in fact, far more complicated than the future of the adjacent Shahjahanabad quarter, with its complex spatial texture and social activity. Being a sometime historian of New York City, I tend to follow, with great interest, the historical circumstances of other "world cities" relative to my own, and to speculate on how the urban trajectories of the twenty-first century will unfold. Such rumination is not easy given the moving targets that encompass the present surge in global urbanization. Delhi is no exception. The entirety of Delhi is complicated—not just Lutyens' Delhi with its obvious historical and representative importance. In this regard, Rana Dasgupta's perceptive study *Capital: The Eruption of Delhi* (2014) is helpful in defining the "paradoxical multitude of authorities" that comprise the Indian political order and the nature of Delhi's "maturity" that differs radically from what we have come to expect of "mature global cities." He astutely warns us of the dangers of oversimplification, that the question "When will Delhi 'grow up'?" is the "tourist's question that very few people in Delhi ask."[1] Presumably for good reason.

Dasgupta looks at the future of Delhi with reference to New York City. He points to a significant difference between twentieth century New York and twenty-first century Delhi. He suggests that a significant difference involves the emerging "deterritorialized" elites in our newly globalizing world—that while New York's old-money elite tended to invest in its own localized future, the circumstance in Delhi is different, entailing a dispersal of local accountabilities. But in twentieth-century New York, it was also true that the city suffered a travesty at the hands of a "deterritorialized" elite as early as 1963 with the destruction of Pennsylvania Station. Perhaps the New York experience can hold promise for twenty-first century Delhi—in that in New York, the destruction galvanized a powerful preservation movement without old money. Perhaps the passing of Lutyens' Delhi will be less violent, though infinitely more complicated. Indeed, New Delhi is already no longer Lutyens' Delhi.

I suppose that in our work, the "tourist's view" is unavoidable.[2] We assume that no one can dispute the need for defensive action regarding the future of Lutyens' Delhi; that one can anticipate a "grown-up" discussion about what happens next; and that, in effect, the question belongs to national and international stakeholders as well as to Delhi. At a minimum, we also assume that with an architectural and planning landmark belonging to the world at risk, "deterritorialization" just might come to its defense, and that international debate is important with or without the local elites. Lutyens' Delhi is definitely under siege by several paradoxical "authorities" as it is an ideologically conflicted remnant of colonial rule, an extremely valuable real estate parcel in the present era of neoliberal opportunism, and a unique piece of urban ecology in a Delhi vastly changed from a century ago. At present, the question of its future does seem to be of global interest as much as local. But as global bystanders, we are forced to speculate on whether or not India will be able to muster an appropriate response to the complex debate, and whether an effective time frame to address the forces at hand can be found.

Our "touristic" view is encapsulated in four provocations that admit to the reality that Lutyens' Delhi is already compromised and highly incrementalized in terms of disposition and causes. Within this context, it is clear that an overall "master plan" would arrive too late to be effectual—the strategy of the "pilot plan" seems more realistic, together with investigation of site fragments that this strategy might assemble under the diverse forces that are coalescing. So our effort points toward rationalizing the present situation with hope for a predictable future. It is place-based research in the sense that specific site studies have driven the overall conclusions. Four site conditions became the catalysts: the Bungalow Zone; the Janpath; the remnants of Baoli, Huyuz, and Nullah; and the adjacent Kidwai Nagar neighborhood. All these sites identify infrastructure as critical to connecting past and future.

Some critics will question whether or not our work goes far enough—that Lutyens' Delhi must be destroyed in order to be saved. Others will argue a strict preservationist line before more is lost. Both stances have some validity. Practical or not, the work assumes that a "benign transformation" can be an option—benign in the sense that the cultural, spatial, and ecological identity of the Lutyens composition can be retained through a controlled process of densification.

1 Rana Dasgupta, *Capital: The Eruption of Delhi,* (London: Penguin Books, 2014), 433.
2 The Spring 2015 Columbia Urban Design Studio was commissioned to work on preservation and densification strategies for New Delhi. Field study was conducted in January 2015 in the context of a rapidly transforming world heritage site.

What We Did

Excerpted from "Introduction: What We Did," *Turgutreis 1974,* coauthored with Suha Özkan (Istanbul: Literatür, 2016).

Turgutreis, Karabağ Village

The research at Turgutreis now spans three generations.[1] In the Turkey of the second half of the twentieth century, a generation is a long time. And perhaps nowhere else in Turkey has a generation of change been more expansive than on the southwest Aegean coast. One can hardly imagine a broader range of transformation than at Turgutreis. Statistics tell a partial story. In 1965, the area at the tip of the Bodrum peninsula that today comprises the study area, contained 2,464 souls clustered in three small villages: Karabağ, Akçaalan, and Karatoprak. Forty years later, there were more than 23,000 year-round and more than 250,000 in the summer. Between 1985 and 1998, the population on the whole of the Bodrum peninsula at the height of development grew by 100 percent—from 37,966 to 75,994 year-round residents, and many more in the summer.

In Turgutreis, a "city" of vacation houses, condominiums, and hotels has appeared where the three small villages previously stood. One might dismiss this development as "normal" and a reflection of a larger phenomenon seen across the Mediterranean. But unlike most locations, what previously existed at Turgutreis survives through our studies. Beyond the statistics, we were able to document the physical and cultural form of the transformation itself, which displaced a localized way of life and building by an entirely divergent ideal. Human faces could be layered over statistics and generalities. What has been impressive is the apparent ease and the rapidity of this process. Perhaps an equivalent transformation occurred in the United States in the industrial urbanization of the first half of the nineteenth century, or even in the post-industrial deurbanization of the first half of the twentieth century. But for both, the equivalent change took several generations. In Turgutreis, we witnessed this change in only one generation, or even less. This temporal compression crossed a threshold that represents a significant escalation in comparison to precedents elsewhere.

The impetus for this research began elsewhere—in the United States, where at the end of the '60s I was caught up in the political movements of that period. I began to investigate an "anthropology" of built form that could contextualize the political struggles within the framework of spatial environmental constraints.[2] The Turkish architect Doruk Pamir, a colleague at Pennsylvania State University, suggested a Turkish study to me as I left for Columbia University. He teamed me with Suha Özkan, then a young faculty member at Middle East Technical University. And in March of 1974, we met in Ankara to begin a rather complex process of deciding on a site. This quest entailed addressing the larger question of what the appropriate problematic was, given the Turkish situation at that moment.

The Turkish situation was complex. By 1974, Turkey was entering the politico-economic storm that led to the military coup of 1980.[3] Underlying much of the political disorder was the divergence of two components of Turkey's modernization project, which had been previously perceived as one and the same: "development" on the one hand, and "Westernization" on the other.[4] Turkey was experiencing the gradual destabilization of old meanings of "Westernization," and by the '70s the term was being intertwined with membership in the "Western Alliance." The changing internal order could not tolerate the political dimension of this distinction. And the Western Alliance itself was shifting such that the nature of Turkey's military importance was diminishing. The rise of a new internal political landscape increasingly jostled the old political mandate for an entirely secular state. At a certain level, the Turgutreis project emerged out of these uncertainties—or more precisely, even, was produced by them.

We agreed to look for a site for an "anthropological" study that could give meaning to the spiraling events. It was a long search that led to Turgutreis. It was to be a textbook case-study. An old culture overshadowed by the touristic appeal of the place once infrastructural investments were complete—principally a new road that would connect to the historically impenetrable interior. This road would forever alter the timeless relationship of the place to the sea, reminding us of Fernand Braudel's "island that the sea does not surround."[5] As a case study, the site seemed ideal—as not only a physical environment but also a social environment—for our objective was to understand a lifeworld on the brink.

By the end of June 1974, the Columbia team had arrived at Turgutreis. Our first view of the peninsula and sea was unforgettable, as we slowly wound down the primitive road from Milas to Bodrum. And more extraordinary still was the first view of the plain of Turgutreis. Before us was the lush green "sea" extending to the coastline and horizon beyond. It was beautiful, but hardly untouched or "timeless." It had a certain vitality. The twentieth century had brought several significant transformations—yet the physical and social environment seemed to retain a continuity with the distant past. The previous thresholds of change dated back to the '20s and '30s. First was the Treaty of Lausanne, the European-mandated "population exchange" of 1923, an attempt to conclude decades of festering turmoil in the region with roots in world conflict. Greeks were expelled from the mainland to the islands, Turks from the islands to the mainland.[6] The division of labor within the local economy was radically altered. Indeed, one could speculate that the '20s represented the most profound diaspora since the third century BC, when Mausolus depopulated the Lelegian cities in the region. With time and new citrus production, the economy recovered—but fifty years later, the social diasporas still remained beneath the surface, not infrequently mentioned by the older residents.

The second threshold came with the transformation of agriculture beginning in the '30s, from the timeless Mediterranean subsistence production of grain and olives, to the tangerine cash crop that was created by new irrigation technology comprised of deep wells and internal combustion pumps. In a short period, the region transformed from one of the poorest on the southwest coast to one of the richest, without external infrastructural development, undue external controls, and interferences. It must be emphasized that this transformation was, by all appearances, a remarkably gentle and sustainable one, at least in comparison to the era of new road infrastructure and tourism that was to come. In 1974 the place was still relatively untouched, but roads were planned and the new municipality, Turgutreis, was in place for purposes that could only foreshadow development. A plan for the "Halicarnassus Seashore National Park" had been prepared to protect that investment, made under the aegis of the United States Agency for International Development and the United States National Park Service.[7]

In the tradition of "place-based" studies, our initial approach was pragmatic and straightforward: to represent the existing material culture of the place such that planning for the transformation could adequately reflect and preserve its character, which would be, after all, the source of its continuing touristic potential. Our approach was to invoke the daily lives of some fifteen families, chosen based on their representative socioeconomic diversity and the geographic distribution of their domestic environments. Our "study" families seemed optimistic for the future. Already relatively comfortable, most of them foresaw further benefit from modernization. New infrastructure was coming—roads and electricity—and the first televisions and refrigerators had already arrived.

Our initial work was seen as bridging the then-contemporary literature by architects related to documentation of "informal" built environments, with heightened interest among anthropologists in the daily life of alternative Western normative cultural settings. Our intention was to redeploy this genre of new "engaged" research toward the exigencies of actual problem-solving, pushed further than Giancarlo De Carlo could manage at Urbino.[8] We sensed that there was something to be addressed relative to the new material culture then just appearing at Turgutreis—in effect the final phase in the "internationalization" of the place, spanning from the period of artificial social partitioning (the Treaty of Lausanne) to the imposed "modern" building tectonic of the Mediterranean tourist economy that was spreading from Spain eastward. We imagined that the "common person" could be represented in this process. In 1974, our families seemed to understand the importance of our task, as the future still represented something new. But over the years, as their fantasy of the future remained unlived, their naive faith evaporated, and our relationship to the social landscape gradually changed, as did the landscape itself.

Having identified the subjects of our study, our fieldwork methodology evolved over the course of the next two months. Our technique focused on the physical documentation of domestic environments and the material culture in general, interrelated with a written social record based on extensive interviews. The graphic representation of the built environment began with field-measured sketches produced by numerous visits to each family and to the other sites under consideration, such as the grain and water infrastructures. These sketches were translated into hard-line architectural drawings (plan, section, elevations, and detail) on site during our two-month stay. At the same time, the families and several other individuals (including Hasan Muslu, the miller) were interviewed extensively. Throughout the process, a lexicon of the idiosyncratic local terminology related to material culture was developed.

During this same period of textual deliberation, we began historical research with the intention of placing the twentieth century developmental thresholds at Turgutreis within the two thousand years of recorded history on the Bodrum peninsula. A certain commonality between graphics and written texts had to be developed—the development of a common nomenclature, for example, for spaces and their implements. A very important aspect of the visual "language" problem had to do with how to render the "softness" of the traditional building forms and tectonic, which were clearly not compatible with the hard-line and hard-edge techniques of modern mechanical drafting. A freehand technique was developed, together with an extensive lexicon of building elements that could be duplicated as needed. In this way the team could achieve a considerable variation within a uniform visual rhetoric.

By 1976, however, the political turmoil in Turkey had already begun to set in, affecting everything. The project faltered and became dormant. The possibility of projecting to a "plan" was erased. Going back to the work a decade later, however, we realized that it had potential other than what was originally intended—as documentation of a moment that, frozen in time, could become a reference for understanding the changes that had since intervened.

We returned to Turgutreis for the first time in 1986, the work now having shifted primarily to Columbia teams. While the place was recognizable, it had already transformed through urbanization and the introduction of the new tourism economy. The original families were by and large still extant in the houses that we knew so well, but their lives had changed beyond what anyone could have imagined in 1974. The people we had interviewed were growing old; their children were coming of age as a very different next generation. The study families remembered what had been, and they began to comprehend the enormity of change that was upon them. They recognized certain advances in the material aspects of their lives, but the optimistic future felt in 1974 remained elusive to many. While the nature of our dialogue with the families changed, a dialogue it still was, at least at the beginning. They valued seeing our many photographs and depictions of their houses, and they appreciated our shared memories of a different time. We went back again in 1990, 1994, and 1997, until the original generation and any meaningful remaining representation of its culture was largely erased. By then, the memory of what once was became very difficult to rehabilitate.

Our visits were not exercises in nostalgia. We became equally fascinated with what was new as with what had disappeared. We constructed a record of the buildout of the new municipality's master plan, which had quickly urbanized 20 kilometers of coastline with hotels and second homes. We were very interested in the new architecture emerging, especially at two scalar extremes: the monumental new urban landscape, and the detailed local modifications to the Mediterranean modern vernacular for new construction techniques. In the new buildings, gone was the sensitivity to the site and climate. Gone were the old house types, which blended social organization with the landscape, and placed a premium on the family as a coherent organism. Instead, the modern Western house emerged both in individual and collective form. It was configured by the concentration of modern service cores rather than by social gathering. Of huge importance was the transition to Western domestic furnishing, which invalidated the spatial typologies of the traditional houses. Equal status was given to private rooms as to public space. The exterior was constrained by discreet outdoor space in the form of the balcony. Within this homogenized urbanization, one could only hope to still find localized particulars related to the public presence of historical continuities. There were precious few, largely *ad hoc,* survivors.

The phenomenon of the Turgutreis transformation and our slowly evolving cognizance of the importance of our growing documentation made it extremely difficult to arrive at an end point. What it all means was difficult to sort out from inside the work—not to mention the difficulties associated with the implicit criticism of our Western enculturalization that the work raises. In a sense, what we documented can be seen to reflect critically on ourselves. We did not succeed in replacing our original goal of producing a "plan" based on our data. And while the project is "anthropological," we are not anthropologists—we could not provide the ingredient of a continuous disciplined academic discourse with which to cloak the raw material of our work. This is not to say that "anthropology" as a formal discipline could not stand to emphasize more engaged applications, but the academic legitimacy for an "anthropology of building," as we liked to call it, could not come just from "architecture." The joining of "anthropology" and "architecture" remains an elusive goal in both the academy and practice.

Each return trip increased the risk of romanticizing what we found in 1974, or of simply indulging a voyeuristic superficiality. We have learned that it is not enough to cite the empty lesson that nothing lasts. Probably my most memorable revisit was the last, in 1998 and without students, when I could reflect on the enormity of what had come to pass, and at the same time, on that change relative to modern transformations everywhere in the world. As I walked up the road to Karabağ, to seek out Ali Karakaş, I was connected to similar phenomena in my childhood in the United States. I realized that perhaps one value of the work is its global connectivity. In 1974, the house of Ali and Zeynep Karakaş had been far from the changes, sited high above it in Karabağ. At that point, Karabağ looked like it must have at the beginning of the fifteenth century when Turgut Reis was born there. Looking at the new urban landscape in 1998, I found it ironic that all this transformation should be made in the name of the famous Ottoman admiral born in the same spot six centuries ago. Modern roads were being superimposed on the maze of old paths and hedgerows, leading high above the village, where pretentious and domineering new villas were popping out of the steep elevation.

It was shocking to see the small house of Ali and Zeynep Karakaş now dwarfed by a huge mound of earth rudely intruding into the yard, as if to express impatience with this remnant of the old order. Zeynep died in 1990, but Ali, by now seventy-eight, had managed to hang on. He was at home and as generous as

125

ever, offering the traditional greeting, *hoşgeldiniz*. He knew why I was back, the limits of language seemingly insignificant. In spite of the yard's disarray, there were still the familiar grapes to be offered from the *ferek*. There was precious little left of what he knew as irrevocable only twenty-five years before. "It is difficult times now," he related. He did not sell his land for new construction. He tried instead to continue with his tangerines, though a blight destroyed them. Gone even were the four chickens that had been present the previous year. He talked most of all about the strangers, of criminality, and immorality. "As the number of buildings increased, adultery increased." I found the metaphor intriguing. When we said goodbye we both knew it was definitive. I looked back.

1 Field study of the urbanization of Turgutreis was conducted in 1974, 1986, 1990, 1994, and 1997, with follow-up Columbia architecture studios and additional field research by the author and Suha Özkan. For the origins of this project, see Doruk Pamir, *Doruk Pamir Buildings / Projects 1963–2005* (Istanbul: Literatür, 2006), 26–27.

2 Richard Plunz, *Mantua Primer: Toward a Program for Environmental Change* (Baltimore, MD: United States Public Health Service, 1970); Richard Plunz, *San Leucio: Vitalità d'Una Tradizione. Traditions in Transition* (New York: George Wittenborn and Company, 1973).

3 For an overview of the political situation that led to the 1980 coup, see Hugh Poulton, *Top Hat, Grey Wolf and Crescent* (New York: New York University Press, 1997).

4 This point is convincingly developed by Atila Eralp in "Turkey in the Changing Post-War World Order: Strategies of Development and Westernization," in *Developmentalism and Beyond. Society and Politics in Egypt and Turkey*, ed. Ayşe Öncü, Çağlar Keyder, and Saad Eddin Ibrahim (Cairo, EG: The American University in Cairo Press, 1994).

5 Fernand Braudel, *The Mediterranean* (New York: Harper and Row, 1973), 160.

6 The local effects of this displacement are well described in Fatma Mansur, *Bodrum: A Town in the Aegean* (Leiden, NL: Brill Publishers, 1972).

7 Milli Parklar Dairesi, *Halikarnassos Sahil Milli Parkı. Uzun Devreli Gelime Planı* (Ankara, TU: USAID, 1972), 15.

8 Giancarlo de Carlo, *Urbino: The History of a City and Plans for its Development*, trans. Loretta Schaeffer Guarda (Cambridge, MA: MIT Press, 1970).

Nesting

Across a broad range of cities, contexts, and cultures, it is possible to identify generic similarities in spatial patterning that transcend the specificities of place and time. Pattern recognition is fundamental to field urbanism, and certain techniques may be roughly modeled following recognition technique in field ecology. The following plates are evidence of this line of research with representative pattern studies that reflect a number of years of seminar work at Columbia. Just as field ecology has fostered advances in ecological science, so does field urbanism connect to the urban sciences. Although the two sciences are not completely analogous, precedents in field ecology have represented an important jumping-off point for our work in field urbanism. Interrogating public space requires negotiating context, both real and hypothetical. Pattern recognition is fundamental to this negotiation, so much so that commonalities spanning the infinite universes of urban variation across cultures and geographies can only be understood within a comparative framework, one pattern to another.

Pattern analysis requires analytic techniques that engage concepts of nesting, which in the fields of both urbanism and ecology have long been deployed, in various forms, as an essential tool.[1] For field urbanism, a conceptual genesis can be traced back to Anaxagoras (c. 510–428 BC), who contributed significantly to the environmentalism that is part of our Western patrimony.[2] In his *Fragments*, Anaxagoras describes the multi-scalar nesting of pattern within pattern:

> …the portions of what is big and of what is small are equal in plentitude, all things would therefore be in everything; nor could there be (complete) separation, but all things have a portion of everything. Since there can be no smallest (piece) to be (completely) separated is not possible, nor coming to be all by itself, but just as in the beginning now too are all things together. For many (portions) are present in all things, equal in plentitude, both in the bigger and the smaller things being separated out.[3]

Leon Battista Alberti in his *On the Art of Building in Ten Books* also famously described the nesting within urban environments in his city/house analogy: "…for if a City, according to the Opinion of Philosophers, be no more than a great House, and on the other Hand, a House be a little City; why may it not be said, that the Members of that House are so many little Houses."[4] Similarly, Henri Lefebvre alludes to the importance of nesting between "Global" (P), "Intermediate" (M), and "Private" (P) components within the context of larger cross-cultural discussions.[5]

The hypothesis for this research is indebted to Anaxagoras, Alberti, and Lefebvre—in understanding the condition of nesting as patterns within patterns. The relationship between city and house is one of nesting; cities also exist within cities and houses within houses. These relationships are multi-scalar, and therefore capable of nesting. Nesting and place are inextricably interwoven to provide the protocols for these studies. At the most basic level, the generation of pattern is the product of compositional invention that is based on empirical evidence gleaned from place.

In modern ecological science, nested hierarchies and systems have provided an operational and philosophical base since Charles Darwin; for ecological taxonomies even longer, since Carl Linnaeus's *Systema Naturae*.[6] For field urbanism, our "systema naturae" engages the classification of building typologies as a key to unraveling the spatial and cultural relationships from which all else is derived. Our place-based windows are Aldo Leopold's "mountain," from which we are able to view both the urban context in its entirety with nested urbanisms scaling up and down, from urban region to house.[7] For our protocols, place begins with the city at large—from which windows are extracted, within windows within windows, to arrive at the definitive scale of granular built form typologies. The windows are the beginning and end points of a multi-scalar forensic process.

Central to pattern interpretation is the construction of algorithms that can lead to numerical/geospatial analogues. When applied in reverse, the algorithms can function as a design tool to generate similar fabrics within the contemporary context of the same or different cities, or to generate alternative fabrics that may better respond to contemporary situations involving similar formal pre-requisites. The analogue is formed through the algorithm and vice versa. The construction of numerical and geospatial analogues for existing fabric types must be derivative in origin, design, and use. Embedded in the analogues must be an algorithmic approach that involves a procedure or formula for achieving the pattern options.

We compare numerous cities relative to their particular characteristic fabric types. To varying degrees, the construction of numerical and geometrical analogues references the processes that produced the original fabric type. These analogues are then applied as tools to explore new syntax that might better respond to contemporary situations involving similar formal prerequisites. These "design" transformations are the final element. The eight plates that follow this afterword represent a sample of forty neighborhoods in thirty-four cities, with their respective "before" and "after" fabrics, as graphic evidence of the complex processes that can be characterized as "deep urbanism."

Our normative window, from which the syntax explorations begin and end, measures 800 by 800 feet at a scale of 1 inch = 40 feet.[8] Our window comprises the area of approximately three and a half Manhattan blocks, in order to provide sufficient granularity in distinguishing the spatial and social fabric of a neighborhood in varied circumstances and cultural origins. The researcher must engage architectonic transformation within the window when considering macro-scale socioeconomic and spatial scenarios. The window transformations are governed by nonspatial and micro-scale elements including socioeconomic typologies. From this world and street view, the algorithm is derived and the analogue future scenarios constructed. The decoding of historical layers is of varying interest and emphasis.

Today's globalizing urban cultures tend to hybridize. Cities with diverse cultural origins may share analogues and fabric types.

Cross-cultural approaches and applications (from one city to another) are useful. Fabric originating in widely variant cities with diverse formal characteristics can be comparatively evaluated. For this reason alone, it is important to understand the precise typological range that may be drawn upon in a given circumstance, through pattern representation that constructs and reconstructs particular historic contexts.[9]

Field urbanism is fundamentally engaged with process and succession. Historical layering is key to understanding succession, and succession lies at the basis of analogue development. In field ecology there are various iterations of succession theory developed since Darwin that are relevant to our purposes.[10] Field urbanism also engages succession models as important tools. For the evolution of urban fabric, Josef Stübben's *Der Stadtebau* (1890) provides an early comparative model of urban fabric patterning.[11] Patrick Geddes' "Valley Section" in *Cities in Evolution* (1915) is an early expropriation of biological analogues for the city-region.[12] For building types, Gianfranco Caniggia's *Lettura dell'edilizia di Base* (1979) contributed a comprehensive approach to understanding buildings as morphologic constructs.[13] Economic investment can be particularly useful. Land use succession provides perhaps the most literal analogues.[14]

The immediate precedent for this research can be traced to Ian McHarg's "method" of landscape analysis, which sought to layer the environment into characteristic pattern types.[15] For built fabric, the work of Serge Chermayeff and Christopher Alexander pioneered digital correlation of pattern layers.[16] Alexander's subsequent research followed these early explorations.[17] The pattern language concept facilitated digitization in that it addressed the need for an intermediary language between actual and virtual. My own field study in Mantua, Philadelphia sought to further this approach through agent-based algorithms for an urban community exhibiting rapid and pathological change characteristics.[18] With the subsequent PC revolution and GIS capabilities, technical facility was increased for layering techniques, but still required the kind of handwork that these eight plates represent. Important to this process are distinctions within "nested-ness," and the hierarchies of nested pattern scales. Also important are the nested subliminal languages, from anthropology, ecology, geography, communication, and whatever else may emerge from our associated urban "banks" and "mountains."

1 For an overview of nesting theory in ecological science, see Edward T. Wimberley, *Nested Ecology: The Place of Humans in the Ecological Hierarchy* (Baltimore: Johns Hopkins University Press, 2009), 141–42.

2 For the historical evolution of environmentalism, see Lester J. Bilsky, ed., *Historical Ecology: Essays on Environment and Social Change* (Port Washington, NY: Kennikat, 1980). In particular, J. Donald Hughes' essay "Early Greek and Roman Environmentalists," 45–59.

3 Anaxagoras, *The Fragments of Anaxagoras*, ed. David Sider (Sankt Augustin, GE: Academia Verlag, 1981), 80.

4 Leon Battista Alberti, *On the Art of Building in Ten Books*, trans. Joseph Rykwert (Cambridge, MA: MIT Press, 1991); in particular, see Book 1 and 9.

5 Henri Lefebvre, *The Production of Space* (Cambridge, MA: Blackwell, 1991), 147–58; also see Neil Brenner, "The Urban Question as a Scale Question: Reflections on Henri Lefebvre, Urban Theory, and the Politics of Scale," in *International Journal of Urban and Regional Research* 24.2 (June 2000).

6 For relevant perspectives on Linnaeus and on the metaphysics of ecological science, see David R. Keller and Frank B. Golley, ed., *The Philosophy of Ecology: From Science to Synthesis* (Athens, GA: University of Georgia Press, 2000).

7 Roderick Nash has been particularly useful in situating Leopold's contribution within the context of North American urbanization. See Roderick Nash, *Wilderness and the American Mind* (New Haven: Yale University Press, 1967).

8 The author first explored "nested" concepts for urbanism in the fall of 1970. See "Course Outlines," in *Richard Plunz Papers 1935-1999*, Avery Drawings & Archives, Columbia University.

9 Donald Worster's writing on environmental history is particularly prescient. See "Appendix: Doing Environmental History," in *The Ends of the Earth: Perspectives on Modern Environmental History*, ed. Donald Worster (New York: Cambridge University Press, 1988). Also see Donald Worster, *The Wealth of Nature: Environmental History and the Ecological Imagination* (New York: Oxford University Press, 1993).

10 Ecological succession has been variously described by Steward T. A. Pickett, sometime collaborator of Columbia University Urban Design Studio. For a record, see Brian McGrath et al., *Designing Patch Dynamics* (New York: Columbia University Graduate School of Architecture, Planning, and Preservation, 2007).

11 For many decades, Stübben's lexicon of urban fabric patterning was a primary resource for spatial planning. See Josef Stübben, *Der Städtebau* (Stuttgart: Alfred Kröner Verlag, 1907).

12 Geddes's valley section concept dates to the 1910 *Cities and Town Planning* exhibition in Edinburgh. See Patrick Geddes, *Cities in Evolution* (London: Williams & Norgate Ltd., 1915), xi–xviii, 163–94.

13 Caniggia's taxonomies for building types remain a principal methodological referent. See Gianfranco Caniggia and Gian Luigi Maffei, *Composizione Architettonica e Tipologia Edilizia* (Venice, IT: Marsilio, 1979).

14 A literal application of natural succession theory is found in Richard B. Andrews, *Urban Land Use Succession Theory* (Madison, WI: Center for Urban Land Economics Research, University of Wisconsin, 1980).

15 See Ian L. McHarg, *Design with Nature* (Garden City, NY: Natural History, 1969). The evolution of McHarg's method is described in Ian L. McHarg, *A Quest for Life: An Autobiography* (NY: Wiley, 1996), Chapter 7.

16 Serge Chermayeff and Christopher Alexander, *Community and Privacy: Toward a New Architecture of Humanism* (Garden City, NY: Doubleday, 1963). This first agent-based digital modeling was run at the MIT Computation Center's IBM 704. Christopher Alexander, *Notes on the Synthesis of Form* (Cambridge: Harvard University Press, 1964).

17 For the most useful of Alexander's several "pattern language" studies for urbanism, see Christopher Alexander, *A Pattern Language: Towns, Buildings, Construction* (New York: Oxford University Press, 1977). The technique made its way into field ecology; see Stephan Harrison, Steve Pile, and Nigel Thrift, ed., *Patterned Ground: Entanglements of Nature and Culture* (London: Reakton, 2004).

18 Richard Plunz, *Mantua Primer: Toward a Program for Environmental Change* (Baltimore, MD: U.S. Public Health Service, November 1970).

Plates

The following plates are representative of research on nesting, made in the seminar "Fabrics and Typologies New York/Global" taught by Richard Plunz between 1993 and 2015. More than 220 sites were analyzed in more than 114 cities.

PLATE 1

Jackson Heights, Queens, New York. 1992. Michael Conard.

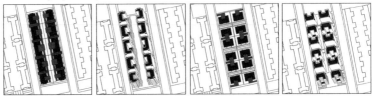

Millbank Estate, Westminster, London, Great Britain. 1992. Andrew Thomson.

Man Cheong, Western District, Hong Kong, China. 1993. Wayne Chang.

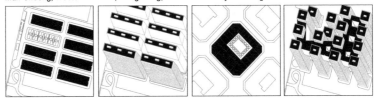

Huanghuo Housing Project, Guangzhou, China. 1994. Eric Epstain, Lin Li, Nils Peters.

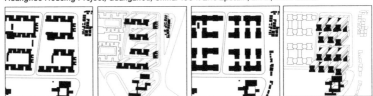

Mid-Wilshire District, Los Angeles, California. 1994. Marc Brune, Euk Kwon, Kevin Tyrrell.

Park Hill One Housing, Sheffield, Great Britain. 1994. Ralf Felmeier, Nathan Ogle.

PLATE 2

South Street Neighborhood, Philadelphia, Pennsylvania. 1999. Earl Jackson, William Kenworthy.

Old Town, Prague, Czech Republic. 2005. Kubi Ackerman, Karin Chen.

Renaissance Center, Detroit, Michigan. 2008. Michael Contento, Jinwoo Heo.

Siemensstadt, Berlin, Germany. 2008. Ariel Hsieh, Hector Lim, Julia Siedle.

Tuscolano, Rome, Italy. 2008. Olympia Cermasi, Nuala Gallagher.

Null Bazaar, Mumbai, India. 2008. Amardeep Labana, Shreya Malu.

PLATE 3

Plaza de San Nicolàs, Havana, Cuba. 2009. Gabriel Fuentes, Joshua Turner.

Sant Pau Barrio, Barcelona, Spain. 2009. Come Menage, Robert White.

Oksu-dong Area, Seoul, South Korea. 2009. Seyoon Kim, Hyo Youn Kwong.

Over-the-Rhine Neighborhood, Cincinnati, Ohio. 2010. Heinz von Eckartsberg, Nathalie Guedes, Joeseph Kirchof.

La Croix Rosse Quarter, Les Minguettes District, Lyon, France. 2010. Jihye Lee, Israel Medina, Amarine Nabi.

Kentron Neighborhood, Yerevan, Armenia. 2010. Heghine Grigoryan, Austin Sakong.

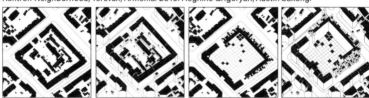

PLATE 4

Nad Al Hamar Quarter, Dubai, United Arab Emirates. 2010. Racha Daher, Jeremy Welsh.

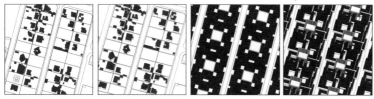

Anarkali Bazaar Area, Lahore, Pakistan. 2010. Jamie Abrego, Fariah Choudhary.

Wan Zhu Jie Street Area, Shanghai, China. 2010. Adriana Amendolara, Ruya Saner.

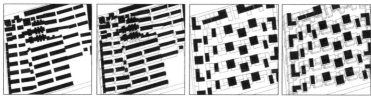

ZAC Massena Nord, Paris, France. 2011. Nefeli Kalantzi, Julie Marin.

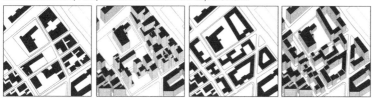

Mokattam Village, Cairo, Egypt. 2011. Guneet Kaur Anand, Tzu-Pei Jeng.

Al Markaziya, Abu Dhabi, United Arab Emirates. 2011. Hannah Allawi, Minyoung Kim.

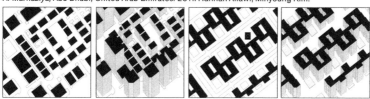

137

PLATE 5

Vakeel Quarter, Shiraz, Iran. 2011. Richard Off, Maryam Zamani.

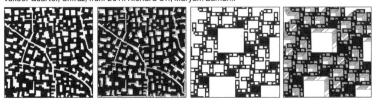

Zion Road HDB, Singapore, Singapore. 2011. Raden Andhini, Aireen Batungbakai.

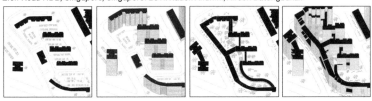

Oksu-dong Area, Seoul, South Korea. 2009. Seyoon Kim, Hyo Youn Kwong.

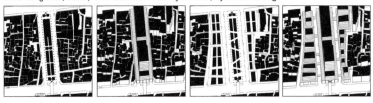

Old North, Saint Louis, Missouri. 2012. Scott Archer, Aaron Foley.

Agios Pavlos (Saint Paul) Quarter, Athens, Greece. 2012. Eleni Gianpapa, Shiyao Yu.

Pesyan District, Tehran, Iran. 2012. Elham Morovvati, Mahrad Shahbazi.

PLATE 6

Tanjong Pagar, Singapore. 2012. Kyng Su Park, Zalina Sapie.

Juer Hutong, Beijing, China. 2012. Xiaokang He, Yuan Ma.

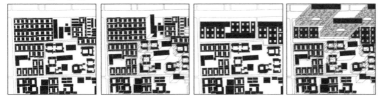

Siemensstadt, Berlin, Germany. 2013. Kirk Finkel, Wagdy Alef Moussa.

Jing'an Village, Shanghai, China. 2013. Ximing Chen, Yili Gao.

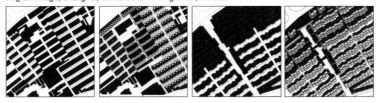

Bukchon, Seoul, South Korea. 2013. Jihan Lew, Taehyung Park.

Shida Night Market, Taipei, Taiwan. 2013. Fan Guo, Yu-Hsuan Lin.

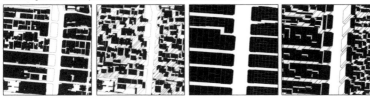

PLATE 7

Hubei Neighborhood, Wuhan, China. 2013. Jing Deng, Wen Wu.

Mong Kok Quarter, Hong Kong, China. 2014. Tin Yan Cheung, Tzu-Yi Chuang.

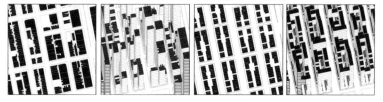

Jianyeli Neighborhood, Shanghai, China. 2014. Hanqing Kuang, Che Wang.

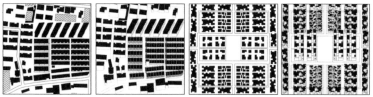

Union Boulevard, Bucharest, Romania. 2014. Cezar Nicolescu, Manole Razvan Voroneanu.

Lexington Terrace, Chicago, Illinois. 2015. Nicolle Rebecca Gitlin, Despo Thoma.

Vieux Carre, New Orleans. Louisiana. 2015. Nishant Samir Mehta, Grace Helen Salisbury Mills.

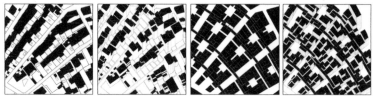

PLATE 8

Pink City, Jaipur, India. 2015. Cameron Dean Cortez, Shiwani Pol.

Old City, Lucca, Italy. 2015. Zyiang Zeng, Guangyue Cao.

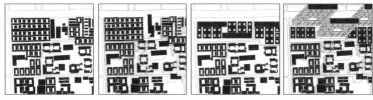

Chinatown, Manhattan, New York. 2015. Chenxing Li, Fei Xiong.

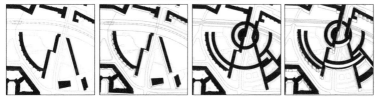

Caoguang Hutong, Beijing, China. 2015. Xi Chen, Jiajing Cao.

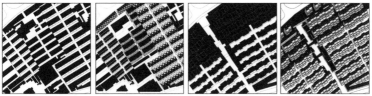

Hubei New Village, Shenzen, China. 2015. Xinye Li, Zhuoran Zhao.

Lajpat Nagar, New Delhi, India. 2015. Surbhi Kamboj, Zhou Wu.

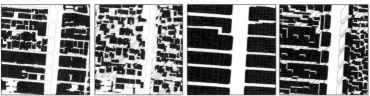

Installation detail from *New York Paleotectonic*, 1995, in the permanent collection of the Queens Museum of Art, 48 × 24 inches. *New York Paleotechnic* was exhibited in "City Speculations," November 16, 1995–March 10, 1996. Collaborators: Richard Plunz, with MSAUD students Victoria Benatar, Maria Fernanda Gómez de Llarena, Hubert Klumpner, and Erich Prödl.

COLUMBIA GLOBAL CITIES STUDIOS

The majority of the texts in this volume grew out of Columbia University Global Studios in Urban Design directed by Richard Plunz from 1993 to 2015. Over forty global cities were studied in collaboration with local government entities, community stakeholders, universities, and other research institutions. Each studio practiced design as a development tool—design as catalyst for the integration of a wide range of disciplines and areas of expertise in urbanism. Faculty participants included: Mojdeh Baratloo, Michael Conard, Amir Pasic, Eric Brewer, Ignacio Lamar, Kate Orff, Mihai Craciun, Kathi Holt-Damant, Choon Choi, Cinzia Abbate, Ana Maria Duran, Victoria Marshall, Ira Mia Jones-Cimini, Brian McGrath, Geeta Mehta, Erich Prödl, Petra Kempf, Vanessa Keith, Alberto Foyo, Shue Tshen, Zhou Conghui, Victor Body-Lawson, Gabi Callejas, Barbara Camus, Juan Esteban Correa Elejalde, Priscila Coli, Seiyong Kim, and Zenobia Meckley.

1993. Antwerp, Belgium: Stuivenberg Rail Yards and Eilandje Dock
Studies focused on the redeployment of obsolete nineteenth-century infrastructure, principally related to rail and dock facilities and their impact on the relationship between the old city and the burgeoning periphery.

Sponsors and Collaborators: Antwerpen 93, European Cultural Capital; City of Antwerp Stad aan de Stroom project.

Exhibited at "Open City" in Antwerp, May 1993 and at the Salon d'Architecture in Antwerp, November 1993; published in *Taking Sides. Antwerp's 19th-Century Belt: Elements for a Culture of the City* (Antwerp: Open Stad, 1993).

1994. London, England: West Silverton Royal Docks
Studies focused on an obsolete nineteenth-century docklands area, approximately 8 kilometers from the center of London. The studio evaluated the goals of the London Dockland Development Corporation plan, which called for development of a mixed-use "urban village," and in response, explored a series of alternative development proposals.

Sponsors and Collaborators: Architectural Association, Housing and Urbanism Program, London; London Docklands Development Corporation.

1994. Antwerp, Belgium: Petroleum Zuid
Studies focused on the Schelde River, a major brownfield site at the southern boundary of the city, and the site of a petroleum storage area with related port and railyard connections. Of all Antwerp's remaining obsolete port areas, the Schelde River is the only significant parcel owned by the city, making it a target for redevelopment.

Sponsors and Collaborators: City of Antwerp Department of City Planning; Van de Velde Instituut, Antwerp; City of Antwerp Department of Town Planning; City of Antwerp Stad aan de Stroom Project; Antwerp Strategic Regional Plan; Katholieke Universiteit Leuven Faculty of Architecture.

Exhibited at "Open City" in Antwerp, June 1994.

1995. Brussels, Belgium: "Manhattan Plan"
Studies focused on several transitional areas around the original historic core of Brussels, including the so-called "Manhattan Plan" adjacent to the North Station—a large "American-style" urban renewal zone that failed financially and programmatically and still remains unfinished.

Sponsors and Collaborators: Katholieke Universiteit Leuven Faculty of Architecture; Van de Velde Instituut, Antwerp; Brussels "Open City" Program; Beurs Schouwburg Cultural Center, Brussels.

Exhibited at "Open City," May 1995 and at Beurs Schouwburg Cultural Centre; published in *A Moving City* (Brussels: Brussels Studio Open City, 1998).

1995. Detroit, Michigan: Central Area
Studies focused on the central area of Detroit, comprising the original Woodward Plan (1807), which at the time remained semi-abandoned and dysfunctional.

Sponsors and Collaborators: Cranbrook Academy of Art; Wayne State University College of Urban Labor and Metropolitan Affairs; University of Detroit School of Architecture; Detroit Historical Society; Detroit Renaissance; Rivertown Group; Detroit Community Development Associates.

Exhibited in "Detroit is Everywhere" at Storefront for Art and Architecture in New York, May 1995; exhibited and presented at the "Spotlight Festival" in Detroit, June 1995; see also "Detroit Is Everywhere," *Architecture* 85 (April 1996): 55–61.

1996. Istanbul, Turkey: Zeyrek
Studies focused on the quarter of the historic peninsula, which faced physical degradation abetted by disinvestment policies, physical isolation with Atatürk Bulari, and a Kurdish majority population living at poverty level.

Sponsors and Collaborators: Research Centre for Islamic History, Art and Culture (IRCICA), Istanbul; Yildiz Technical University Faculty of Architecture; Faculty of Architecture, Mimar Sinan University Department of City and Regional Planning; Municipality of Fatih, Istanbul.

1996. Caracas, Venezuela: Cota Mil
Studies focused on the completion of the Cota Mil highway connection to La Guaira through a large area of barrios and explored the maximization of highway use as a positive force for community redevelopment.

Sponsors and Collaborators: Regional Institute for Urban Studies (IREU); Municipality of Libertador, Caracas; Office of the Governor, Federal District, Caracas.

Exhibited at the Venezuelan Cultural Center Symposium in New York, December 1997; published as *New Urbanisms 2: Caracas La Cota Mil* (New York: Columbia University Graduate School of Architecture, Planning, and Preservation, 1998).

1997. Brussels, Belgium: Thurn und Taxis
Studies focused on the reuse of the abandoned Thurn und Taxis rail freight terminals, a World Monument site occupying a strategic position at the center of the city.

Sponsors and Collaborators: Beursshouwburg Cultural Centre, Brussels; Brussels "Open City" Program; Katholieke Universiteit Leuven, Instituut voor Stedebouw en Ruimtelijke Ordening; La Fonderie, Brussels; Port of Brussels.

Presented at "Open City" in Brussels, October 1997.

1997. Caracas, Venezuela: Barrio Lidice
Studies focused on a detailed strategy for the Barrio Lidice, the location of a proposed highway bridge completing the Cota Mil highway connection to La Guaira.

Sponsors and Collaborators: Regional Institute for Urban Studies (IREU); Centro Simón Bolivar, Caracas; Universidad Central de Venezuela Instituto de Urbanismo; Universidad Metropolitana Faculty of Architecture; Universidad Simón Bolivar Faculty of Architecture; Centro Cultural Consolidado, Caracas; Centro Cultural La Estancia, Caracas; Concejo Municipal Caracas; Guradia Nacional, Caracas; Venezuela Ministerio de Desarrollo Urbano; Museo de Arte Contemporaneo de Caracas Sofia Imber (MACCI); P.D.V.S.A.; Policia Tecnica Judicial, Caracas; Consulate General of Venezuela, New York; Avensa Airlines; Soloviajes C.A., Caracas.

Exhibited at Palacio del Gobernacion in Caracas, June 1997; published as *New Urbanisms 2: Caracas La Cota Mil* (New York: Columbia University Graduate School of Architecture, Planning, and Preservation, 1998).

1997. Naples, Italy: Centro Direzionale
Studies focused on the "Centro Direzionale" development adjacent to the Central Station, designed by Kenzo Tange in the 1970s. The site remains unfinished and financially unsustainable, and the strategies for its completion need to be significantly reconsidered.

Sponsors and Collaborators: Consorzio Gestione Servizi Centro Direzionale; University of Naples, Faculties of Architecture and Urban Planning; City of Naples.

Exhibited at Refetorio di San Lorenzo in Naples, October 1997; published as *New Urbanisms 1: Naples Centro Direzionale* (New York: Columbia University Graduate School of Architecture, Planning, and Preservation, 1997).

1998. Mostar, Bosnia: "Front Line"
Studies focused on the reconstruction of Mostar in the wake of the Bosnian war, with particular emphasis on the area of the "front line," between the Bosniak and Croatian sectors of the city, to redefine a multi-cultural city.

Sponsors and Collaborators: Mostar 2004 organization; Mayoralty of the City of Mostar; Research Centre for Islamic History, Art, and Culture, Istanbul; Aga Khan Trust for Culture, Geneva; Institute for Preservation of Cultural Heritage, Mostar; World Monuments Fund, New York; Fundacio Bancaixa, Spain; Ajuntament de Barcelona, Districte 11.

Presented in Mostar to the organization Mostar 2004, July 1998; published as

New Urbanisms 3. Mostar: Bosnia & Herzegovina (New York: Columbia University Graduate School of Architecture, Planning, and Preservation, 1998).

1999. Mexico City, Mexico: Water Urbanism
Studies focused on the transformation of the ecology of Mexico City, and the possibilities of remediation oriented urban strategies, related to the hydrology of informal settlements.

Sponsors and Collaborators: Universidad Nacional Autonoma de Mexico (UNAM) Faculty of Architecture; Direction General de Construccion Hidraulica; Distrito Federal (Mexico City).

2000. Prague, Czech Republic: Prague 13
Studies focused on the further urbanization of the Prague 13 district, the largest Soviet-era housing estate within the metropolitan region, including strategies for diversifying both the urban fabric and local enterprise.

Sponsors and Collaborators: Municipality of Prague 13; Office of the Lord Mayoralty of City of Prague; Prague City Development Authority; Prague 2000 European City of Culture organization; U.S. Embassy, Prague.

Exhibited at Czech Center in New York, June 2000 and at the "City of Culture" program in Prague, November 2000; published as *New Urbanisms 5: Prague 13* (New York: Columbia University Graduate School of Architecture, Planning, and Preservation, 2000).

2001. Caracas, Venezuela: El Litoral
Studies focused on the reconstruction of 90 kilometers of coastline destroyed by the mudslide disaster of December 1999. Strategies included large-scale infrastructural planning and small-scale barrio reconfigurations.

Sponsors and Collaborators: Colegio de Arquitectos de Venezuela, Caracas; Fundación de Arquitectura y Diseno Urbano (FADU), Caracas; Universidad Central de Venezuela, Caracas; Globovision, Caracas; Instituto de Patrimonio Cultural, Caracas; Instituto Regional de Estatios Urbanos, Caracas; Universidad Metropolitana, Caracas; Universidad Católica Andres Bello, Caracas; AUAEV, Caracas; CONAPRI, Caracas; Fundación Armando y Anala Planchart, Caracas; Fondación Plan Estrategico de Caracas; Fundación Venezolana de Investigaciones SismologicasVenezuelan (FUNVISIS); Regional Institute for Urban Studies, Caracas; Ministerio de Infraestructura, Caracas.

Published as *New Urbanisms 6: Litoral Central, Venezuela* (New York: Columbia University Graduate School of Architecture, Planning, and Preservation with Princeton Architectural Press, 2005).

2002. Belgrade, Serbia: Post-Soviet Urbanism
Studies focused on the evolution of the Post-Soviet city and urban territories of Communist-era formation, with particular emphasis on the "formal" and "informal" economic sectors as development tools.

Sponsors and Collaborators: University of Belgrade Faculty of Architecture; National Office for Spatial and Urban Planning, Republic of Serbia; Agency for Building Land and Construction of Belgrade; Ministry of Transport and Telecommunications, Republic of Serbia; Town Planning Institute of Belgrade; U.S. Embassy, Belgrade

2003. Larderello and Val di Cecina, Italy: Geo-Thermal Urbanism
Studies focused on geothermal energy as a source for physical and economic infrastructural reconfiguration, including tourism and settlement patterns within the framework of the western Tuscan landscape.

Sponsors and Collaborators: ENEL Green-Power, Rome; "La Sapienza" University, Rome Faculty of Architecture, Department of Urban and Regional Planning; Geothermal Museum, Larderello; Mayoralties of Pomarance, Castelnuovo, Val di Cecina, Montecatini; Directorate of the Val de Cecina Mountain District; University of Florence Faculty of Architecture.

Published as *New Urbanisms 7: Geothermal Larderello: Tuscany, Italy* (New York: Columbia University Graduate School of Architecture, Planning, and Preservation, 2005).

2003. Bangkok, Thailand: Water Urbanism
Studies focused on the changing relationship of water to urban infrastructure, including the obsolescence of the canal urbanization, regional hydrological characteristics, and issues surrounding large-scale infrastructural disruptions.

Sponsors and Collaborators: Chulalongkorn University Faculty of Architecture, Bangkok; Bangkok Metropolitan Authority; Thai National Environmental Board.

2004. Brisbane, Australia: Density Proxemics
Studies focused on the generative effects of passenger rail investments on regional

urban patterns with an emphasis on densification patterns.

Sponsors and Collaborators: University of Queensland School of Geography, Planning, and Architecture; Queensland Rail; Queensland Transport; Brisbane City Council; Gold Coast Council.

Published in *Emerging Urban Futures in Land-Water Infrastructure* (New York: Columbia Graduate School of Architecture, Planning, and Preservation, 2009).

2004. Bucharest, Romania: Density Proxemics
Studies focused on emerging developmental infrastructure within the metropolitan region of Bucharest, related to post-Soviet reconstruction and to areas of new construction within the new economy.

Sponsors and Collaborators: "Ion Mincu" University of Architecture and Urbanism, Bucharest; City of Bucharest Department of Urbanism; Romanian Ministry of Transport; CasaNATO; U. S. Embassy, Bucharest.

2005. Barcelona, Spain: L'Hospitalet d' Llobregat
Studies focused on economic and physical development of L'Hospitalet, a peripheral municipality of Barcelona, due to its increased regional significance relative to expanding transport infrastructure (air, road, and rail).

Sponsors and Collaborators: Municipality of L'Hospitalet d' Llobregat, City of Barcelona Sector for Urbanism; Consorcio Gran Via; Urban Land Institute Spain; Universitat Politècnica de Catalunya.

Exhibited at L'Hospitalet d' Llobregat Symposium in Barcelona, January 2006.

2006. Seoul, Korea: Cheonggyecheon River
Studies focused on secondary development impacts along a one kilometer section of the Cheonggyecheon River restoration project to form a nexus for consolidation of growth in the expanding metropolis.

Sponsors and Collaborators: Korean Institute of Architects (KIA); Korea University School of Architecture (SAKIA); Urban Institute of Korea (UDIK); Konkuk University School of Architecture, Department of Environmental Engineering; Chung-Ang University.

2006. Rome, Italy: Corviale
Studies focused on the Corviale Housing project—the longest single housing block

in Europe spanning one kilometer—with the aim of redesigning and integrating the project into the surrounding urban context and examining its role as a peripheral edge condition in the expanding metropolis.
Sponsors and Collaborators: Faculty of Architecture, "La Sapienza" University, Rome; Lazio Department of Regional Planning; Lazio Housing Authority (ATER); Municipality of Rome.

Published in *A Research for Corviale* (Rome: Casa Editrice Università degli Studi di Rome La Sapienza, 2006).

2007. Quito, Ecuador: Quebrada Urbanism
Studies focused on stabilizing static conditions and retrofitting infrastructure in informal steep slope settlements.

Sponsors and Collaborators: Corporácion Vida Para Quito, Municipalidad de Quito; Empresa Municipal de Alcantarillado; Facultad de Arquitectura, Deseño y Artes, Pontifica Universidad Católica del Equador (PUCE).

2007. Guayaquil, Ecuador: Mangrove Urbanism
Studies focused on the remediation of dispersed informal sea-level settlement intrusions through consolidation and densification.

Sponsors and Collaborators: Municipalidad de Guayaquil; Facultad de Arquitectura y Deseño, Universidad Católica de Santiago de Guayaquil; Colegio de Arquitectos del Ecuador and the Bienal de Arquitectura de Quito.

2008. Bangkok, Thailand: Carbon Urbanism
Studies focused on detailed design investigations of the infrastructural and fabric upgrades along the Khlong Phadung Krung Kasem Canal, including the Hua Lamphong Rail Station, and considered strategies for carbon neutral development and redevelopment in the city.

Sponsors and Collaborators: Chulalongkorn University Faculty of Architecture, Bangkok; Bangkok Metropolitan Authority.

Published as *The Carbon Studio: Bangkok* (New York: Columbia University Graduate School of Architecture, Planning, and Preservation, 2008).

2009. Vienna, Austria: 22nd District Hausfeld
Studies focused on modes of development and spatial infill in the eastern periphery of Vienna, the site of extensive new

infrastructural investments, including a new metro connection and redevelopment of the abandoned Aspern Airfield.

Sponsors and Collaborators: City of Vienna Urban Development and Planning Department; 2008 European Year of Architecture.

Published as *Aspern Vienna: Scenarios for Development* (New York: Columbia University Graduate School of Architecture, Planning, and Preservation, 2009); and *Entwerfen Für Das Hausfeld: Designing Housfeld* (Vienna: Municipality of the City of Vienna, 2009).

2009. Mumbai, India: Dharavhi
Studies focused on infrastructural retrofitting and upgrading within the largest informal settlement in India, including research into strategies for the next generation of economic development.

Sponsors and Collaborators: Partners for Urban Knowledge, Action, and Research (PUKAR); Society for the Promotion of Area Resource Centres (SPARC).

Published as *Mumbai Dharavi: Scenarios for Development* (New York: Columbia University Graduate School of Architecture, Planning, and Preservation, 2009).

2010. Mumbai, India: Eastern Docklands
Studies focused on repurposing the eastern port area of Mumbai and integrating it into the surrounding urban fabric.

Sponsors and Collaborators: Mumbai Port Trust; Kamala Raheja Vidyandhi Institute of Architecture (KRVIA); Urban Design Research Institute (UDRI); JJ School of Architecture; URBZ: User Generated Cities; Institute of Public Policy, New Delhi; Partners for Urban Knowledge, Action, and Research (PUKAR).

Published as *Mumbai Eastern Waterfront: Development Transects* (New York: Columbia University Graduate School of Architecture, Planning, and Preservation, 2009).

2010. Kingston, Jamaica: Downtown Port
Studies focused on the port harbor and its associated shoreline, looking primarily at the Downtown Port rejuvenation and its effect on the surrounding commercial and residential development.

Sponsors and Collaborators: University of West Indies (UWI); Kingston Restoration Company (KRC); Urban Development Corporation (UDC); National Environment

and Planning Agency (NEPA); Jamaica National Heritage Trust.

Published as *Kingston Harbor: Development Transects* (New York: Columbia University Graduate School of Architecture, Planning, and Preservation, 2010).

2011. Gulin, People's Republic of China: New Town
Studies focused on the design development of New Town adjacent to the existing historic city with a particular emphasis on innovation in green infrastructure, housing diversity, and public space hierarchies.

Sponsors and Collaborators: Gulin County Central Communist Party; Central Academy of Fine Arts, Beijing; Columbia University Beijing Global Center; Earth Institute Urban Design Lab.

Published as *Gulin New Town: An Integrated Design Framework* (New York: Columbia University Urban Design Lab, 2011).

2011. Kharkov, Ukraine: Inner Periphery
Studies focused on the nineteenth-century inner periphery of the city suffering from disinvestment, infrastructural obsolescence, and economic disjunction in the new post-Soviet economy.

Sponsors and Collaborators: Kharkov Regional Administration; Department of Urbanism and Architecture, and Chief Architect of Kharkov; Kharkov State Technical University of Construction and Architecture; Roddom Institute.

Published as *Urban Strategies for a Post-Soviet Kharkov* (New York: Columbia University Graduate School of Architecture, Planning, and Preservation, 2011).

2011. Accra, Ghana:
Ga Mashie and Nima East
Studies focused on upgrading the infrastructural and housing fabric in the Ga Mashie and Nima East communities of Accra, with emphasis on multi-scalar techniques for deploying incremental investment.

Sponsors and Collaborators: AMA (Accra Metropolitan Assembly); GAMADA (Ga Mashie Development Agency); University of Ghana at Legon; Earth Institute Millennium Cities Initiative.

Published as *Urban Development in Accra, Ghana* (New York: Columbia University Urban Design Lab, 2011).

2012. Kumasi, Ghana:
Adukrom-Akrom-Sawaba and Bantama
Studies focused on basic infrastructural development and built fabric densification in three rapid-growth peripheral areas and on the provision of social services within the inner city context.

Sponsors and Collaborators: Kumasi Metropolitan Assembly (KMA); Departments of Planning and Architecture, Kwame Nkrumah University of Science and Technology; Department of Women, Regional Ministry, Ashanti Region; Kumasi Metropolitan Education Department; Kumasi Metropolitan Health Department; Bantama Sub-Metro Authority.

Published as *Re-Cultivating the Garden City of Kumasi* (New York: Columbia University Urban Design Lab, 2012).

2012. São Paulo, Brazil: Itaquera
Studies focused on infrastructural upgrades in an area of the city under intense development pressure catalyzed by new transit and World Cup infrastructure.

Sponsors and Collaborators: São Paulo Secretary of Housing (SEHAB, HABI and COHAB – São Paulo's Housing Company); Secretary of Urban Development (SMDU, SP Urbanismo), Secretary of Parks and and Environment (SMVMA); School of Architecture and Urbanism, University of São Paulo (FAU-USP)

Published as *Madureira, Rio De Janeiro & Itaquera, São Paulo: Comparative Informalities* (New York: Columbia University Urban Design Lab, 2012).

2012. Rio de Janeiro, Brazil: Madureira
Studies focused on the rationalization and preservation of the flourishing commercial center under intense development pressure.

Sponsors and Collaborators: Rio de Janeiro Heritage Department (SUBPC); Rio de Janeiro Secretary of Housing / Programa Novas Alternativas (SMH); Port Area Development Company (CEDURP); Studio-X Rio de Janeiro

Published as *Madureira, Rio De Janeiro & Itaquera, São Paulo: Comparative Informalities* (New York: Columbia University Urban Design Lab, 2012).

2013. Vienna, Austria:
11th District Simmering
Studies focused on existing planning initiatives within Vienna's new urban "ring," exploring alternatives for urban infill and the effects of the large-scale infrastructural investments currently underway in the city.

Sponsors and Collaborators: City of Vienna Urban Development and Planning Department.

Published as *The Middle of the Fields: In der Wiesen Mitte* (New York: Columbia University Urban Design Lab, 2013).

2013. Bordeaux, France: Rocade Ring Road
Studies focused on innovative approaches to envisioning the Rocade 2030 with particular emphasis on the mutation of urban fabric and infrastructures within numerous ongoing urban projects and strategic studies.

Sponsors and Collaborators: Communauté Urbaine de Bordeaux (CUB) Urban Dynamics Department (A'Urba); Bordeaux School of Architecture (EnsapBx); Arc en Rêve (Bordeaux Center for Architecture).

Published as *Peripheries in Transition: Bordeaux 3.0 and The Rocade* (New York: Columbia University Urban Design Lab, 2013).

2014. Kisumu, Kenya: Manyatta
Studies focused on infrastructural upgrades to the growing informality in Manyatta, in response to development pressure from the adjacent downtown area with an emphasis on preserving and enhancing the lifestyle and cultural assets of its current residents.

Sponsors and Collaborators: Earth Institute Millennium Cities Initiative; Earth Institute Urban Design Lab; Catholic Organization for Relief & Development Aid (Cordaid); Maseno University; Municipal Council of Kisumu (MCK).

Published as *Spatial Strategies for Manyatta: Designing for Growth* (New York: Columbia University Urban Design Lab, 2014).

2014. New Delhi, India: Lutyens Plan
Studies focused on the question of new alternatives to urban fabric infill in New Delhi's sparsely populated ceremonial core, preserving the character and amenities of the original plan for the national capital.

Sponsors and Collaborators: School of Planning and Architecture; New Delhi Municipal Committee (NDMC); Delhi Urban Arts Commission (DUAC); Indian National Trust for Art and Cultural Heritage (INTACH).

Exhibited at Steelcase Asia Pacific Holdings in Gurgaon, Delhi, January 2015; published as *Reimagining Lutyens' Delhi*

149

(New York: Columbia University Urban
Design Lab, 2014).

2014. Medellin, Colombia: San Cristobal
Studies focused on alternatives for
consolidation of pari-urban growth
through identification of urban centralities
and the reduction of urbanization pressure
on land considered valuable for other
uses, including new forms of agricultural
production.

Sponsors and Collaborators: Faculty of
Architecture, Universidad Pontificia
Bolivariana; Earth Institute Urban Design
Lab; Institute for Metropolitan and Region-
al Studies, Department of City Planning
of Medellin; Agency for International
Cooperation of Medellin and Antioquia.

2015. Seoul, South Korea: Suwon City
Studies focused on the investigation
of replacement functions for several large
national government facilities being relo-
cated to other cities with consideration
of knitting new functions into surrounding
contexts and expanding their economic
base.

Sponsors and Collaborators: Mayor and
Municipal Government of Suwon City;
Low Carbon City Project, Center for Urban
Regeneration and Education (CURE),
Korea University; Graduate Urban Design
Program at Korea University; Korean
Planners Association.

Exhibited at Suwon City Hall in South
Korea, October 2015.

2015. Rio de Janiero, Brazil: Santa Cruz
Studies focused on the critical evaluation
of current models for urban growth in a
fast-developing peripheral urban sector
with adequate infrastructural capacity and
on the related diverse challenges from
this, ranging from environmental remediation to housing typologies to public space.

Sponsors and Collaborators: City Administration of the *Sub-Prefeitura* of Santa Cruz;
Strategic Planning Advisory Board of Rio;
Santa Cruz Core of Historic Guidance
and Research (NOPH); Graduate Program
in Urbanism, Federal University of Rio
(PROUB).

SELECTED ADDITIONAL TEXTS SINCE 1992

"Waiting for the Other Shoe to Drop.
Het Nieuwe Amerikaanse Getto." *Archis*
(October 1992).

"Water and Development in Manhattan."
In *Waterfronts. A New Frontier for Cities
on Water,* edited by Rinio Bruttomesso,
311–31. Venice: International Center Cities
on Water, 1993.

"On the Uses of Air. Perfecting the New
York Tenement, 1850–1901." In *Berlin /
New York. Like and Unlike,* edited by Josef
Paul Kleihues and Christina Rathberger,
159–79. New York: Rizzoli, 1993.

"Zoning and the New Horizontal City."
In *Planning and Zoning New York City:
Yesterday, Today and Tomorrow,* edited by
Todd W. Bressi, 27–47. New Brunswick,
New Jersey: Center for Urban Policy
Research Press, 1993.

"Richard Plunz" (interview). In *Roma,
New York, Moscow,* edited by Alessandra
Latour, 182–84. Rome: Edizioni Kappa,
1993.

"Een Dokter Voor de Staad" (interview with
Paul Blondeel). *De Standaard Magazine,*
July 30, 1993.

with Janet Abu-Lughod. "The Tenement
as a Built Form." In *From Urban Village to
East Village,* edited by Janet Abu-Lughod,
63–79. Oxford: Blackwell, 1994.

"Beyond Dystopia. Beyond Theory Formation." In *Mortal City,* edited by Peter Lang,
28–35. New York: Princeton Architectural
Press, 1995.

"New York Paleotectonic: 1964–95." In *City
Speculations,* edited by Patricia Phillips,
68–71. New York: Princeton Architectural
Press, 1996.

"Introduction," In *Naples: New Urbanisms:
Centro Direzionale.* MSAUD New Urbanisms.
New York: Trustees of Columbia University,
1997.

"Several Cities and a Few things to be Said
About Them." *Domus* 809, November 1998.

with Michael Sheridan. "Deadlock Plus 50.
On Public Housing in New York," *Harvard
Design Magazine,* Summer 1999.

"After Salt: Circumnavigating the Theme of Taboo." *After Salt: Master Class in Architecture,* 19–26. Salzburg: Internationale Sommerakademie für Bildende Kunst, 1999.

"Roads and Development." In *Two Adirondack Hamlets in History: Keene and Keene Valley,* edited by Richard Plunz, 49–96. Fleishmanns, New York: Purple Mountain Press, 1999.

"Urban Intellectuals in the Valley." In *Two Adirondack Hamlets in History: Keene and Keene Valley,* edited by Richard Plunz, 191–237. Fleishmanns, New York: Purple Mountain Press, 1999.

with Viren Bharmbhatt. "De-Masking the Mont des Arts: Panorama Populaire." In *Vacant City: Brussels Mont des Arts Reconsidered,* edited by Bruno DeMeulder, 306–313. Rotterdam: NAI Publishers, 2000.

with Iñaki Echeverría. "Beyond the Lake: A Gardiner's Logic." *Praxis* 2 (2001).

"City: Culture: Nature: The New York Wilderness and the Urban Sublime." In *The Urban Life World: Formation Perception Representation,* edited by Peter Madsen and Richard Plunz, 45–81. London: Routledge, 2002.

"*Community and Privacy*—and Chermayeff's Impatience About Idiots." In *Fejder: Studier i Stridens Anatomi i det Intellectual liv,* edited by Frederik Stjernfilt, Frederik Tygstrup, and Martin Zerlag. Copenhagen: Museum Tusculanums Forlag, 2004.

"L'Hospitalet Será El Brooklyn Catalán" (interview with Lluis Amiguet). *LaVanguardia,* January 21, 2006.

"History of Public Housing in New York." In *A Research for Corviale,* edited by Anna Irene del Monaco, 99–93. Rome: Casa Editrice Università degli Studi di Rome La Sapienza, 2006.

with Maria Paola Sutto. "Re-Centering Around Climate." *Domus* 930, November 2009.

with Petra Kempf. "Positioning the Periphery: 'Vienna Outside-In'." In *Entwerfen für das Hausfeld: Designing Hausfeld,* edited by Erich Prödl and Richard Plunz. New York: Columbia University Urban Design Program, 2009.

with Kubi Ackerman. "Managing and Modeling Fluvial Systems: Ongoing Projects at the Urban Design Lab." In *Emerging Urban Futures in Land-Water Infrastructures: South East Queensland,* edited by Mojdeh Baratloo and Kathi Holt Damant, 80–91. New York: Graduate School of Architecture, Planning and Preservation of Columbia University, 2009.

"The Design Equation: Landscape in a New Key." *Landscape Architecture China* 13, no. 5 (2010): 37–45.

"Endgame: In the Bubble: New York City Housing Production, 1978–2008." *Lotus International* 147 (September 2011): 90–103.

"The Urban Design Equation." In *Rebooting Urban Design: Energy, Economy, Ecology,* edited by Mojdeh Baratloo, 10–15. New York: Graduate School of Architecture, Planning and Preservation of Columbia University, 2013.

"Notes on a Saturday along Madrid Rio." In *Landscapes in the City: Madrid Rio: Geography, Infrastructure, and Public Space,* edited by Francisco Burgos, Ginés Garrido and Fernando Porras-Isla Editors, 276–77. New York: DAP Distributed Art Books, 2014.

with Patricia Culligan. "Group-form and Urban Infrastructural Resilience: New York City as an Example." In *Cities in the 21st Century: Academic Visions on Urban Development,* edited by Oriol Nel-lo and Renata Mele. London: Taylor and Francis, 2015.

INDEX

Note: Page numbers appearing in italics refer to illustrations.